To my father,

Who put sand in my shoes, a pack on my back,
and led me into the woods.
There are lessons to be learned among the trees,
he said.

CONTENTS

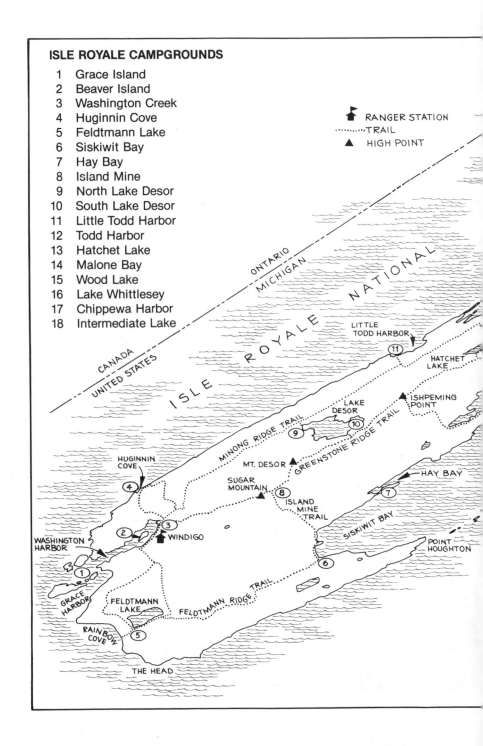

ISLE ROYALE CAMPGROUNDS

1 Grace Island
2 Beaver Island
3 Washington Creek
4 Huginnin Cove
5 Feldtmann Lake
6 Siskiwit Bay
7 Hay Bay
8 Island Mine
9 North Lake Desor
10 South Lake Desor
11 Little Todd Harbor
12 Todd Harbor
13 Hatchet Lake
14 Malone Bay
15 Wood Lake
16 Lake Whittlesey
17 Chippewa Harbor
18 Intermediate Lake

RANGER STATION
TRAIL
HIGH POINT

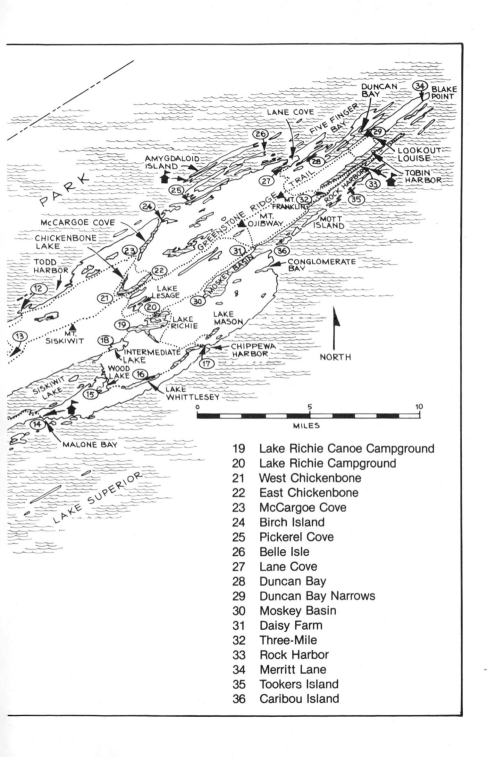

19 Lake Richie Canoe Campground
20 Lake Richie Campground
21 West Chickenbone
22 East Chickenbone
23 McCargoe Cove
24 Birch Island
25 Pickerel Cove
26 Belle Isle
27 Lane Cove
28 Duncan Bay
29 Duncan Bay Narrows
30 Moskey Basin
31 Daisy Farm
32 Three-Mile
33 Rock Harbor
34 Merritt Lane
35 Tookers Island
36 Caribou Island

FOREWORD

As the first Island National Park, Isle Royale occupies a special niche in the National Park System. The remoteness that inspired the vision of the early National Park supporters is as much a part of the wilderness experience today as it was in 1931. Isle Royale is the classic National Park, a complete, self-contained ecosystem buffered and protected from most outside influences by the clear waters of Lake Superior. It is a place where man is only a temporary visitor for a short time each year, permitting the natural system to grow and develop with little human influence. Visitors to Isle Royale are given the opportunity to enjoy both exquisite beauty and natural integrity in one place. What one takes away from the Island is limited only by one's imagination and willingness to prepare for the experience.

This new publication on the foot trails and water routes of Isle Royale National Park provides a wealth of information and insights for Island visitors. It is the first comprehensive hiking and paddling field guide to Isle Royale, and Jim DuFresne has done a masterful job of making it come alive. His extensive experience hiking, kayaking, and camping on Isle Royale is written from a visitor perspective, making it especially valuable as a field guide. Additional editing and research by Steve Maass, long-time Park employee and Island resident, does much to enrich the publication and ensure the accuracy.

I am certain that this book will quickly become the Bible for wilderness users of Isle Royale. The comprehensive nature of the publication will be a delight to first-time visitors and make their experience richer and more rewarding. Returning visitors, whether on foot or by water, will find the detail and accuracy invaluable. It is with great pleasure that I welcome this new book to our library of Isle Royale literature.

Donald R. Brown
Superintendent
Isle Royale National Park

Painted turtle sunning at Chickenbone Lake.

SPECIAL NOTES

All mileage given in this book is based on the latest records of the National Park Service. They may not coincide with those sign posts in the park that are outdated because of rerouted trails.

Hikers are encouraged to use the standard Isle Royale Topographic Map published by the U.S. Geological Survey. It is sold in the park and through mail-order by the Isle Royale Natural History Association.

Likewise, hikers should consult the most recent edition of the park's Hiking/Camping Brochure for changes in regulations and policy. This is available free by writing the Superintendent, Isle Royale National Park, 87 N. Ripley St., Houghton, MI 49931.

Directions in this book are given as if Isle Royale trended due east and west; strictly speaking, it is oriented northeast and southwest. Hikers, rangers, and the National Park Service speak of Windigo as being at the west end and Rock Harbor at the east end of the island. To avoid confusion, this guide uses those directions.

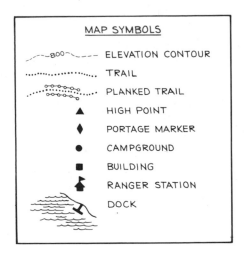

ACKNOWLEDGMENTS

Like those before me, I, too, have fallen in love with the Island. I first arrived with my father at the tender age of nine, and, despite my limited outlook on life, could sense something special about Isle Royale.

My latest trip was a six-week kayaking and hiking expedition in 1982, when I explored the park's most hidden corners—and everything in between. The adventure was one of the best I have ever undertaken, but the highlight occurred afterward. Nothing could give an author more joy than my opportunity to write about the wilderness I have cherished since owning my first pair of hiking boots.

Within these pages, between the descriptions of trails and water routes, are some of my memorable moments from that trip—but only some. For it would be impossible to recall all of them; just as it would be impossible for me to acknowledge everybody who helped me undertake the adventure and complete this book.

My sincere thanks to the National Park Service at Houghton, Michigan and Isle Royale for helping put together what to me was a once-in-a-lifetime experience. Superintendent Don Brown, Stu Crow, Larry Wiese, Craig Axel, and Bruce Weber gave me information, knowledge, and their fondest memories of the park—especially Weber and the Isle Royale Natural Historical Association, who encouraged me to write this book from the beginning.

In the back country, Dr. Rolf Peterson gave me his time and the answers to my questions on the special wolf–moose relationship; and Malone Bay ranger Russ Wilson came up with some duct tape to help me out of a bind with a broken rudder. The trail-crew members, whom I met from one end of the park to the other, gave me some warm laughs on a chilly night.

Thanks also to Steve Maass for contributing his own back-country experiences to the book; to Karen Kangas, the camp-store clerk, who greeted me with a clean towel and ice-cream bars every time I passed through Rock Harbor Lodge; and to my wife Peggy for paying the bills while I spent six carefree weeks in the woods and who then cleaned up the first draft of this book.

Finally, to all the backpackers and paddlers I spent quiet evenings with across the Island, thank you for your suggestions and surplus supplies. This one is for all you bug-bitten lovers of Isle Royale.

j.d.

Shoreline at Malone Bay Campground.

PART ONE

ISLE ROYALE:
THE NATIONAL PARK

Sam Rude's fish camp, Fishermans Home Cove.

1 THE ISLAND

He calls it the Island. The old lake captain, Roy Oberg, does. He has no need to waste his breath on saying "Isle Royale National Park."

The Island tantalized him long before it was a park. Its rugged beauty and suspension of time was a mystic charm that had him returning summer after summer ever since he was a boy: "Way bee'fore them park rangers ever set foot here," he will say proudly.

Isle Royale has a history of that. It has long been a sparkling gem, tempting all who pause in the stormy northwest corner of Lake Superior. Four thousand years ago, pure copper lying exposed between layers of rock lured man across the open water. Later, in the 1800s, it was the good fishing off the shores and reefs that kept him coming back. The moose arrived at the turn of the century, seeking dry land after a frigid swim of 15 miles from the Canadian mainland. In 1949, the wolf journeyed across frozen Lake Superior, seeking out the moose.

Today the Island's attraction is neither copper, easy fishing, nor moose meat. It is something entirely different. In a bustling world of jet planes, cars, flashing neon signs, and news every hour on the hour, Isle Royale is a secluded wilderness. It is a roadless, McDonald-less, slow-changing place where at times you can actually hear...nothing. Not a sound.

Those are rare and valuable qualities in an age when man's ability to lose himself in the woods is rapidly shrinking. Those are qualities that pull 15,000 visitors to Isle Royale every summer. Some of them arrive to stay in the park hotel at Rock Harbor Lodge. Others rarely step off their cabin cruisers, desiring only to fish offshore for lake trout.

But the majority (park authorities estimate anywhere from 9000 to 12,000 visitors) fall into that category labeled "backpackers" by the Park Service. They are canoeists, hikers, and kayakers who live in the city but long for the woods—people who want to surround themselves with wilderness; with spruce trees, wildflowers, and clean air. Rarely does the Island disappoint them.

They begin arriving in mid-May. They are gone by mid-October. Come winter, Isle Royale is the only national park in the country to close down completely. No hikers, no tourists, no fishermen, or hotel employees; empty except for a few researchers and park rangers who keep tabs on the moose and wolves. Closing down for the winter is the only way to preserve the park's final and perhaps greatest asset—land not marred by man's heavy footprint.

To many it is impossible to sit in a hotel room or on the deck of a boat and experience Isle Royale's richest offering. To enjoy the back country, they have to travel to the back country. They seek the exhilaration of hauling a 30-pound pack over a new trail. They cherish a private encounter with a moose and her calf feeding in a beaver pond.

For those who desire this type of escape and vacation, the Island is well suited. The park, small by National Park Service (NPS) standards, is 45 miles long and 8.5 miles wide at its broadest point, comprising more than 210 square miles of wilderness. Its backbone, the Greenstone Ridge, climbs three times to more than 1300 feet, with Mount Desor the highest point at 1394 feet.

Within this area are 170 miles of trails that range from a well-defined hike along a level path to an up-and-down struggle over the Minong Ridge. You could arrange anything from a series of day hikes out of Rock Harbor Lodge to a two-week trek that circles the park and never back-tracks a single step.

The vast majority of trails within the park are well marked and have been planked. Park rangers refer to the numerous wooden walkways that cross wet lowlands as planking and urge hikers to use them. Not only do they keep your boots dry but they prevent the delicate swamp areas from turning into mud baths.

Seventeen portages connect nine lakes, with dozens of coves, harbors, bays, and isolated areas that neither hikers nor powerboaters can reach. You take your pick: Isle Royale's back country on foot or by paddle.

No matter whether you explore by boot or by boat, your first trip to the national park often leaves you planning your second. The mystical pull of the Island has a habit of luring people back to its shores. For in this wilderness, only the moose and wolves can stay.

ISLE ROYALE: HISTORY OF A WILDERNESS

The Island was born during Precambrian time, some 1.2 billion years ago. Lava seeped up through cracks in the Superior Basin and formed basalt, the bedrock of the area. After each lava flow, wind and rain carried sand, gravel, and other sediments into the area, producing slabs of soft rock between the hard layers of basalt.

But the Island's distinct "washboard" appearance—ridges and valleys extending from one end of the Park to the other—was formed when the center of the Superior Basin began to subside. This raised and tilted the layers of rocks on Isle Royale, the Keweenaw Peninsula, and much of the outer rim of the lake. The result was ridges with a steep northwest side and a gradual southeastern slope. Over thousands of years the softer layers of sandstone eroded to form valleys and lakes. The bands of basalt with-stood forces of nature to become the ridges that hikers struggle over every summer.

Glaciers added the final touch to Isle Royale's appearance. Four major ice sheets pushed their way down from Canada and scoured the land as far south as the Ohio River. The last glacier advanced to the Lake Superior area only 11,000 years ago. When it melted, Isle Royale, as we know it to-day, appeared. The glacier's depressions on the land became lakes, coves, and harbors. The rock debris that it had scraped up and pulverized were left behind as a thin layer of soil. When the ice melted as the glacier retreated, the water filled Lake Superior.

It was not long after the final glacier retreated that life appeared on the

Island. Wind and water carried algae that took hold in wet places and lichens that could live on bare rock. Gradually, grass and other higher plants arrived and gained a foothold in the thin layer of glacial soil.

Grass and shrubs carpeted the barren ridges and prepared Isle Royale for the first animals. Birds and airborne insects easily reached the Island. A handful of caribou ventured across the frozen Lake Superior. Hawks, owls, and possibly even a few wolves soon left their home in Canada and were lured 15 miles southeast to the new land.

That was Isle Royale about 10,000 years ago: a subarctic grassland with dwarfed birches and willows and wandering caribou. But as the climate continued to warm, the Island continued to change. Forests replaced the grasslands, and mammals such as beaver, snowshoe hare, and marten appeared along with amphibians, reptiles (such as the painted turtle), and various species of fish that thrived in the inland lakes.

But some animals never made the crossing from the Canadian mainland. Notably missing were black bears, raccoons, porcupines, and whitetail deer.

Inevitably, man finally arrived. He had reached the north shore of Lake Superior by 7000 B.C. and could easily view the Island off in the distance. To the first Indians Isle Royale was the "floating island" and had mystic qualities when the early morning fog made it appear to rise above the water.

We don't know when they made the 15-mile trip from Canada, but we have evidence that they were regularly mining copper by 2000 B.C. The metal was worth making the hazardous Lake Superior crossing. The Indians used a variety of beach cobbles to pound out the pure copper. They fashioned it into knives, spearheads, and ornaments that were traded as far away as New England and Mexico.

Although the Indians' activity peaked between 800 and 1600 B.C., it is believed that their settlements on Isle Royale were rare. Other than hundreds of shallow mining pits, the Indians left few signs of their habitation—unlike their white brothers who followed them to the Island.

Legends of pure copper reached white explorers late in the seventeenth century and prompted the French to explore western Lake Superior. The French gave the Island its formal name and included it on their earliest maps of the giant lake.

Benjamin Franklin may also have heard of the copper-rich island and insisted in the Treaty of Paris (1783) that the boundary between the fledgling United States and England's Canada be drawn north of Isle Royale. Other historians believe the United States ended up with the Island not through shrewd diplomacy, but rather from a mapmaker's error that put the international boundary north of it. Although Isle Royale is much closer to Minnesota, Michigan was given control in 1837, when it became the first Lake Superior territory to be admitted to the Union.

Fishermen used the Island as early as 1800. Isle Royale was ideal, with its long shoreline, many reefs, and wide range of water depths that supported such desirable species as lake trout and whitefish. A small Indian fishing camp still remained at Belle Isle when the Northwest Fur Company sent fishermen to the north shore in the early 1800s.

In 1837, the American Fur Company built a fishing camp on Belle Isle and within two years had seven camps and a crew of 33 fishermen. The largest camp, on Siskiwit Bay, had a storehouse, salt house, a cooper's shop, and a barracks. When the company ceased operation in 1841 because of the economic depression of 1837–1841, fishing remained as an enterprise for individual fishermen. It would prove to be the most enduring commercial activity on the Island.

For a short spell, fishing took a back seat to another enterprise. In 1844 the Chippewa Indians signed a treaty with the United States, giving up their claims to the land. That opened up the Island to full-scale prospecting for minerals. Miners arrived in three waves, with the first lasting from 1843 to 1855. The miners filed claims immediately after the treaty was signed and by 1846 had created a small copper rush to the Island. Although much exploration took place, little metal was ever obtained. The remains of two mines from this era can still be seen: Smithwick Mine, a fenced-in excavation on the Stoll Trail near Rock Harbor Lodge; and the Siskiwit Mine, a marked area on the Rock Harbor Trail between Three-Mile and Daisy Farm campgrounds.

Crude mining methods and Isle Royale's isolation made it almost impossible for the numerous companies to turn a profit. By 1855 the last of

A mining family at Windigo, about 1892. (Fisher Collection photo, Michigan Technological University Archives)

them had ceased operating. But the demands of the Civil War raised the price of copper, and by 1873 there was new interest in what was beneath the rocky surface of Isle Royale.

This time there were fewer but better-financed companies, using advanced techniques. Gone were the methods of finding copper veins by searching rock outcrops or burning away the underbrush. Instead, trained mining engineers and geologists used diamond drills to seek out the mineral. Reliable transportation in the form of lake steamers also aided the mining.

The result was several large mining adventures, including the largest at Minong Mine on McCargoe Cove. Hundreds of nearby Indian mining pits attracted the miner's interest in the ridge, and in 1875 they began to build a mining community. At its peak in the late 1870s, the Minong mining town was home for 150 workers and their families. It included a dock and warehouse at the mouth of McCargoe Cove for lake steamers, an office building, store, school house, and various houses. The miners also constructed a stamping mill, dam, and a railroad, from the dock to the mine site, that required a full-time blacksmith to shoe the horses used to pull the ore cars.

Off of Siskiwit Bay was Island Mine, the site of the other major mining effort of the time. When 80 men reported to work in 1873, the Island Mining Company decided to lay out a township on the north side of the bay. They then built a two-mile road from the bay to the inland mines. During the next few years the company sank three shafts, one 200 feet deep, and constructed a sawmill, dock, and workers' quarters.

The two mines' prosperity, although short-lived, led to a demand of self-government among the workers. Isle Royale County was established in 1875 with Island Mine being the county seat and the Minong settlement a separate township. But poor deposits and falling copper prices ended another spell of mining in the early 1880s.

The final fling at mining occurred in 1889 when investors from England were persuaded to finance another search for profitable copper. This time they looked at the west end of the Island. The town of Ghyllbank was built at the present site of Windigo and included a two-story office building, store houses, and sheds. The mining community numbered 135, including more than 20 children; two babies were born on the Island in the winter of 1890-1891. A second settlement was built two miles inland for workers and single men.

Although miles of roads were built (one as far east as Lake Desor) and extensive diamond drilling carried out, no copper of profitable quantities was ever found. Thus ended the mining era on Isle Royale, a 4000-year stint that produced many artifacts and relics of man's existence—but little metal.

But commercial fishing had remained. It reached its peak in the 1880s with almost 30 fishing camps scattered along the shoreline, including a year-round settlement at Chippewa Harbor. But there was a noticeable drop in the number of whitefish caught in the late 1890s, and fishing began its decline. The creation of a national park in the 1940s hindered the industry, as rangers, enforcing the policy of the times, uprooted many fishermen, who did not own land and burned their camps. Many fishermen had moved on anyway because of depressed fish prices, smaller catches, and opportunities to move to more profitable locations.

Disaster struck in 1952 when the first sea lamprey appeared in Lake Superior. The parasite, which attaches itself to a fish and sucks out the blood and body juices, almost wiped out the lake trout and drove most of the remaining licensed fishermen out of business. By 1972, though the sea lampreys had been controlled, only four fishing permits were left on the Island. Today the fishing industry still exists on Lake Superior but is only a remnant of its glorious height in the late 1800s.

Tourism would blossom in the twentieth century. By 1870 a trickle of tourists arrived on excursion boats to picnic near the site of Siskiwit Mine or the Rock Harbor lighthouse. But with the growth of midwestern cities in the early 1900s, tourism on Isle Royale boomed. The Wendigo Copper Company, unable to find any copper, began to mine tourists. Duluth businessmen built the exclusive Washington Club on the mainland, and Captain Singer of the White Transportation Line built Singer Resort, which featured a bowling alley and a dance hall, on nearby Washington Island. Seven other resorts catering to passengers on the Great Lakes' steamers

Commercial fishery, Chippewa Harbor, about 1892. (Fisher Collection photo, Michigan Technological University Archives)

CCC crew building Mott Island dock, 1938. (National Park Service photo)

were built, including one on Belle Isle that boasted a fine dining room, shuffleboard courts, and even a pitch-and-putt golf course.

At the same time people began to buy islands and plots of land, particularly in Tobin Harbor, for summer homes. By 1920 there was a movement underway to turn the Island into a national park. The man given most credit was the journalist Albert Stoll, Jr. Stoll visited the Island in the 1920s and then wrote a series of articles for the *Detroit News,* promoting national park status for Isle Royale. Congress passed a bill in 1931 making Isle Royale a national park project, and the Island was formally proclaimed a national park in 1940.

Today Isle Royale is one of our smallest national parks and one of the most costly to visit. Special transportation needed to get there, which encourages visitors to stay longer, and the large number of backpackers gives the park one of the longest visitation averages (the amount of time a visitor stays) in the country. Tourists spend on the average only a few hours at Yellowstone National Park, but they will stay three or four days at Isle Royale.

It is only right. For people go to Isle Royale not to sightsee but to escape. They don't merely want to see the wilderness but to experience it—impossible in a two-hour visit. To fully appreciate and understand Isle Royale you must grab your paddle or your hiking boots and wander off for a week or more into the tranquility of its woods.

Only then will the shores of the Island beckon your return.

2 WILDFLOWERS TO WILDLIFE

It was a simple imprint on wet mud. No more than three inches long. One track in perfect form. But it was enough to make me drop my pack, study it on my hands and knees, and send my mind reeling.

It was a wolf track. Sometime after the morning rain, the predator had passed through. It is extremely rare for a hiker to see a wolf in the summer. But they are there, moving in the shadows of the underbrush, watching from afar. You do not see them, but at times you can sense them.

One track is all that is needed. One track is enough to give the park an aura of wilderness, where man and beast are on equal footing.

The Island is truly. . . an island. The expanse of Lake Superior has given it both solitude and protection. From wildflowers to wildlife, Isle Royale has endured the modern world. Despite man's appearance, life on the Island still turns in its natural cycles. There is harmony between plants and animals, between predators and prey, between life and death. Man visits and occasionally rearranges a few pieces, but never has he changed the rules of the game.

This is what makes Isle Royale unique: an absence of outside influence on the behavior of animals and plants. The Island is "penned in" by Lake Superior, which hinders most immigration and emigration of additional species. The Island also has fewer species than the mainland. Many animals never made the crossing after the last glacier scraped the Island clean 10,000 years ago.

Add man's own dedication not to interfere with the natural cycles, and you have animals and plants that behave and live in the most pristine manner. You have the perfect outdoor laboratory. That is truly rare today, so rare that the United Nations recently designated Isle Royale as an international biosphere reserve to promote further scientific study.

THE FAUNA

Much of the research revolves around the wolf. Unlike its other habitats in northern Minnesota or Alaska, on Isle Royale the wolf is controlled not by man's encroaching presence but its own social behavior and the availability of moose—its food source during much of the year.

The wolves strengthen the moose herd by helping to thin out those unable to survive the harsh winter—the old, the sick, and the young. It's an ancient predator–prey cycle. But a strong adult moose has little to fear from a pack of wolves. Its flashing hoofs are protection enough. Thus, the size and condition of the moose herd help determine the growth of the wolf packs.

Other factors—alternate food supplies, weather, and the mortality rate of the newborn—also play a hand in the survival of each species. But

There are about 1000 moose on Isle Royale.

there is little doubt that one without the other would create havoc on the Island.

This was proven at the turn of the century. Faced with growing competition for food on the mainland, the first moose swam to Isle Royale around 1900. Here the moose found an abundance of shrubs and no natural predators. The new herd exploded in numbers, and by 1930 there were an estimated 1000 to 3000 moose on the Island.

The herd began to fluctuate wildly. In the winter of 1933, a large number starved to death. The great fire of 1936, which burned twenty percent of the Island, created vast open areas for small trees and shrubs to take root. The new source of "moose salad" caused another upswing in population.

The boom-and-bust pattern might have continued, but nature finally brought a predator to the Island. Around 1949 a few wolves crossed the 15-mile ice bridge from the mainland and found a ready food supply. Within eight years an estimated 15 to 25 wolves lived in the park.

The relationship is pure and very special to scientists who began studying it in 1958. During the summer, researchers hike around the park collecting moose carcasses to determine the cause of death and to search for signs of wolf activity and pup production. In the winter a small team spends six to eight weeks in the park counting wolves and moose by aerial observation.

Researchers now believe that the moose and wolf predator–prey relationship fluctuates within a 25-year cycle. Within that period, the increase in the number of one species causes a delayed increase in the other. As the number of moose increases, for example, so does the number of moose vulnerable to the wolves, which in turn increases the size of the wolf pack. Gradually, the pendulum swings the other way. In 1980, the wolves on the Island reached an all-time high of 50 animals in 5 territorial packs. Just 2 years later the number had dropped to 14, with only 4 of them traveling in a pack. There were 23 in 1983.

This led to changes in the moose population. In 1977, less than 600 moose lived on the Island. By 1983, the herd had increased to more than 900. Researchers are confident that the number and size of the wolf packs will follow, the way nature intended.

If you have arrived to see a wolf, chances are you will leave Isle Royale disappointed. Only a few lucky hikers ever get a glimpse of one. During the summer the wolves turn to beaver as well as moose for their food source; they stay in the isolated sections of the park, avoiding almost all contact with people. If camping or hiking around the Feldtmann Lake area, you can often spot their tracks in the nearby swamps. And a small number of visitors will hear them howl at night, an eerie bark that is rarely forgotten. Despite all the trails that crisscross the Island, the wolf still has its solitude on Isle Royale.

The moose are a different story. Spotting the ungainly animal that can exceed a height of 7 feet and weigh more than 1000 pounds is easy in the back country. During the summer, moose feed on white birch and aspen in the forest and aquatic plants in streams, lakes, and beaver ponds.

Although you could spot one virtually anywhere, even at Rock Harbor Lodge, they seem to frequent Lake Richie, Feldtmann Lake, Lake Whittlesey, and Grace Creek. A good trail to hike for spotting bulls and cows is Minong Ridge; its ruggedness reduces the number of hikers who might use it. Washington Creek, however, is the easiest place to see one. During the calving season a few cows with their newborn often seek the human activity at Washington Creek Campground because they know the area will be free of wolves.

Park rangers warn visitors that the moose should be treated with caution and never molested—especially the bulls, which can be temperamental during the summer and during rutting season in the fall. Many experienced backpackers rate the moose as the most dangerous animal in North America and the source of even more unpleasant confrontations than the bear.

Visitors should avoid upsetting any wildlife in the park or disturbing or touching their homes or nests, or disrupting their daily activities. The worst thing a backpacker can do is feed any animal, even a camp fox. This only

Beavers create ponds that provide food sources for the moose.

upsets the balance of their natural food chain and makes them dependent on man and his leftovers.

But viewing wildlife on the Island is often the highlight of any trip, and one creature you can watch for hours is the beaver. Once almost extinct, the beaver is now found in large numbers on the Island and plays an important role in the moose-wolf relationship. The ponds the animals create are a source of food for the moose, and the beaver is dinner for the wolves. An estimated 1900 beavers inhabited the park in 1974, and today their distinctive lodges can still be seen along almost any trail.

The lodges are built of sticks and mud and usually house a breeding pair and three or four young. In the summer they feed on aquatic and leafy vegetation, but during the rest of the year they turn to twigs and the inner bark of aspen and birch. A beaver will let you know when you have paddled into its "territory" on an inland lake. The animal will approach your boat to within five or six feet and then slap the water with its tail as it dives below. When done unsuspectingly from behind, it's enough to make you drop your paddle.

Hikers will also spot red foxes during their stay, even if they hike no farther than Daisy Farm Campground. In recent years, the carnivore has become used to man, and now every campground seems to have its own "camp fox" making daily rounds for handouts. In the wild, the fox feeds on squirrels, hares, fish, and berries and often during the winter scavenges on the remains of wolf-killed moose.

Camp fox, looking for a handout. (Photo by Steve and Carol Maass)

Foxes can be a nuisance in the back country because they rummage through packs and supplies left outside the tent at night. More than one hiker has awakened in the morning to find his or her food spread over the campground. For this reason park rangers recommend that food be carried into the tent at night or covered with tarps and sticks. They also warn not to feed foxes, which thereby become more dependent on humans.

Other commonly seen mammals are hares and red squirrels; mink, otter, muskrat, and various species of bat are on the Island but are hard to spot.

The western painted turtle and the common garter snake are usually the only reptiles hikers spot. The most common amphibians in the park are the American toad, the spring peeper tree frog, and the green frog.

Because they are so mobile, a variety of birds can be found in the park— more than any other vertebrate—and encounters with them are inevitable. The most captivating, especially for canoeists and kayakers, is the loon. The common loon, with its distinctive laugh, can be heard throughout the Island, and unwise paddlers often play a game of "hide and seek" with the pairs they encounter on the lakes. This practice is discouraged because it may harm the young.

Other waterfowl that will be seen frequently are the Canada goose, mallard, American black duck, bufflehead, and the distinctive common and red-breasted merganser. Isle Royale also has an abundance of woodpeckers, chickadees, warblers, thrushes, kingfishers, and various species of gulls. Along the shoreline the herring gull is the predominate species, but an occasional Bonaparte's gull can also be seen.

THE FLORA

The part of nature hikers usually study the most on Isle Royale are the trees. Thick forests blanket the Island from Windigo to Blake Point and are broken up only by scattered lakes, swamps, and stretches of rocky ridges. The trees vary in density and variety, but they are always there, crowding the trail and shielding the wildlife community.

Forests on the Island, like wildlife, grow in cycles. When fire or wind creates new open areas in the vegetation, the first seedlings to take root are paper birch, aspen, and, sometimes, jack pine and various willows. These trees can tolerate the warm and usually drier growing conditions to form a successional forest.

If the seedlings are not overbrowsed by moose the forest will grow quickly and create a thick canopy, shading the ground. Paper birch and aspen seedlings find it hard to survive in the new conditions. But other trees do not, and they form the climax forests that gradually replace the successional ones.

The modifying effect of Lake Superior creates the ideal conditions for the first climax forest. The lake water keeps the summers cool and the winters mild along the shore. White spruce and balsam-fir seedlings find these cool, moist, and shaded surroundings ideal. Spruce-fir climax forest exists along the periphery of the park and over much of the interior.

But inland, where the terrain is broken up by ridges, the climate is warmer and drier than that along the shore. These conditions support a climax forest of sugar maple and yellow birch. The tops of Mount Desor and Sugar Mountain (hence its name) are almost pure stands of sugar maple, and maple–birch forests range inland a few miles out of Windigo along the Greenstone Ridge, past Ishpeming Point.

When a destructive force such as wind or fire again destroys part of the climax forest, the cycle is completed. The new open areas attract aspen and paper-birch seedlings, and a successional forest takes root.

In between the two climax forests are transition zones where yellow birch, jack pine, or aspen is dominant. And in swamps and bogs black spruce and northern white cedar thrive.

The best way to see and understand the park's succession of trees is to hike the Island Mine Trail from Siskiwit Campground. The trail begins at the western end of the bay in cool, moist, spruce-fir climax forest, dips into swamps of white cedar and black spruce, and then gradually climbs through a transition forest of spruce, fir, maple, and yellow birch. Eventually, the trail ends at the top of the Greenstone Ridge, where only sugar maple and yellow birch can be found.

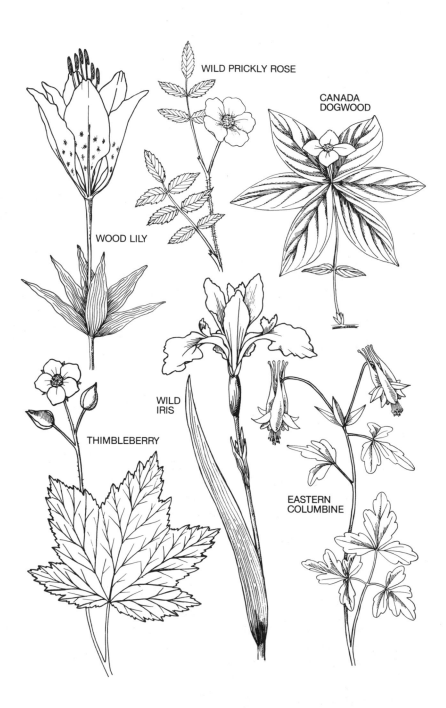

WILD PRICKLY ROSE

CANADA
DOGWOOD

WOOD LILY

WILD
IRIS

THIMBLEBERRY

EASTERN
COLUMBINE

Eastern tiger swallowtail butterflies near Chickenbone Lake shoreline.

Hikers along the trails spend most of their time looking at trees. But it is the wildflowers that catch their eye and break the green monotony of the forest. The wildflowers on the Island are incredible. An official park publication lists 101 kinds, most of which bloom later in the summer than those on the mainland.

Flowers also tend to bloom first at the west end of the park (at Windigo) and gradually ripple eastward toward Rock Harbor. When hiking in late June and early July backpackers heading east are often blessed with a rainbow of flowers along the trails.

The most impressive display of wildflowers occurs in open areas, where late bloomers such as the wood lily are not crowded out by tree seedlings. In swamps, it is common to see the purple wild iris, large skunk cabbage, yellow pond lily, or white wild calla.

On the ridges the hiker will encounter massive growths of western thimbleberry with its white flower, reddish wild prickly rose, or white upright bindweed, also known as the dwarf morning glory.

In the forest is the common Canada dogwood, American starflower, and the hard-to-find yellow lady slipper. The most common berries are blueberries, dwarf raspberries, thimbleberries, and strawberries.

Northern pike—the prize of Island fishing.

3 ISLAND FISHING

The conversation should have been about lakers. When fishermen think of Isle Royale the thought in most minds is a 20-pound lake trout, taken deep in the ice-cold water of Lake Superior.

The fish stories being spun in the ranger's cabin should have been about the fish that was the cornerstone of the Island's great commercial fishing industry in the late 1800s. It would have been proper to pay it homage. Seven of us were sitting in a ranger's kitchen–bedroom–living room, watching a trail-crew member turn a mountain of freshly caught lake-trout into a platter of golden nuggets. We were getting set to eat lake trout, but we were talking pike—northern pike—the sportfish that rules the inland lakes of Isle Royale.

"Lakers have the reputation," said the back-country chef, without taking his eyes off the large cast-iron fry pan where he was performing his magic. "But pike have the fight."

If anybody knows about such things, the Isle Royale trail crews should. They are the highway department of the NPS, brushing back trails, building bridges, and planking swamps in the Island's back country. They work 10-day shifts in the woods, moving through the park by paddling one inland lake after another. Fishing isn't a recreational activity with them, it's a necessity. The more fish they catch, the less food they have to purchase from mainland suppliers.

That day they did quite well. The 6-man crew caught 6 lake trout, all over 22 inches, in Siskiwit Lake by surface trolling with ¾-ounce Daredevils and Little Cleos. Because of their fine luck that day, we were having a feast that night.

The room was filled with the aroma of fried trout, and the air was getting sticky with pike stories. The pike's fierce reputation is built around powerful lunges and a wide mouth armed with rows of sharp teeth. It will eat any animal it can swallow and attack almost anything that moves in the water. In its belly you might find the remains of perch, walleye, lake trout, another pike, or even a small waterfowl. Somebody tells about the series of pike marks he found on the last 8-pounder he pulled in, saying it's common for one large pike to lunge at the side of another passing through.

Eventually, of course, somebody tried to pass along a story of a pike attacking the leg of a hiker wading near the shore of Lake Ritchie. Fierce and crazy, that's how they describe pike on the Island.

"Pike!" said the trail crew member turned chef, "that fish is a freshwater barracuda."

With that he sat down at the table with a plate of trout. The conversation suddenly halted. Everybody had stampeded to the stove for some fish.

Fish fries are a common thing for trail crews and rangers at the national park, because fishing in the inland lakes is largely unspoiled and uncrowded. Only a dozen of the 42 named lakes contain no sportfish; the rest support such species as lake, brook, and rainbow trout, yellow perch, walleye, and pumpkinseed sunfish. But pike is king and the most widespread, thriving in 29 of the park's lakes.

Although an annual migration of powerboaters trolls the outside shore and reefs for lake trout, the number of lines dipped into the lakes are relatively few in comparison. But nobody expects the action on the inland lakes to increase: Two natural barriers keep the number of fishermen limited and the catches large. The first barrier is Lake Superior. The fact that you can't drive to the park and fish from the front seat of your car has always kept the number of anglers down.

The second barrier is the inland lakes themselves—and their inaccessibility. Once on the Island, there is no shortcut to reach them, only the traditional way—on foot. That, more than anything, will always ensure light fishing within the park.

Shore fishing from the trails is productive but restrictive in the number of lakes you can get to. The best way to fish the inland lakes is to *portage* a boat in—no ordinary task. *Portaging* means carrying your boat overland from one body of water to another. The most common boat in the park is the canoe, but some anglers prefer to pack-in a small, two-man rubber raft; a few like to carry a kayak over the trail.

No matter what is used, you first have to carry it in before you can paddle it out. The system of 17 portages ranges from a 75-yard hop, skip, and a jump at Pickerel Cove to a 2-mile grunt between Moskey Basin at the end of Rock Harbor to Lake Richie. Some backpackers prefer to carry a canoe in pairs. But the most common method, either for canoe or kayak, is to attach a yoke over the top and flip it upside down on the shoulders of one person. With your head deep inside, you struggle down the trail, balancing the boat and bumping the trees.

Few people can go more than a half mile without giving their shoulders and back an extended rest. Even fewer people are lucky enough to carry their boat and gear in one trip. Portaging means returning to the original departing point for a second trip to haul what was left behind.

At times portaging is work, at times it is a grunt. But the results are being able to fish sections of the park that hikers can't get to—and pike, trout, or perch sizzling in a pool of butter at dinner time.

Lake Richie is usually the first happy experience backpacking anglers have on Isle Royale. The deep lake, one or two day's travel from Rock Harbor Lodge, supports large populations of pike and yellow perch. Hikers can follow a trail around the northern edge of the lake and reach many weed beds where pike like to hide out.

But those who haul a boat over the trail have the entire lake to fish. The best spots in Richie tend to be the shallow water between the islets and the southern arm that leads off to Chippewa Harbor. Use spoons or plugs of almost any color and cast among the weeds and marshes. And be ready. Pike often follow the spoon right to the side of the boat or the shoreline before taking the lure with a smashing strike.

Siskiwit Lake, the largest—with a length of 7 miles and a depth of 142 feet—contains the best variety of sport fish, including the only inland population of lake trout. Lakers up to 10 pounds are frequently caught in the lake, along with perch, rainbow and brook trout and, of course, pike. Best of all, powerboats are not allowed in the lake. There is a water-taxi service (see Chapter 4) to Malone Bay Campground, an easy 0.2-mile portage from Siskiwit.

Chickenbone, Livermore, and LeSage are a series of lakes in the central part of the park that have excellent foot and portage access. All three are productive spots for pike and perch, and Chickenbone also boasts of walleye. Foot trails follow much of the west end of Chickenbone, part of the north end, and touch a section of the south side.

Isle Royale also offers the other extreme. For those willing to work, a number of isolated lakes provide a rare fishing experience of having a lake to yourself. They are hard to reach either by foot or by boat and thus see little action during the summer.

Lake Whittlesey is known for good-sized pike and the best walleye population on the Island. Pike will hit spoons and plugs of almost any color and type, but walleye present a challenge for the skilled fishermen. Most are taken by slow trolling in early morning or by bobbing a weighted jig off the bottom of the lake. Getting to Whittlesey may be almost as hard as landing a walleye. One route to the lake is to paddle to the western end of Chippewa Harbor and then portage the 0.5-mile trail into Whittlesey. The other is to paddle and portage in from Wood Lake.

Getting a boat to Feldtmann Lake is equally challenging. It requires paddling Lake Superior, either south from Windigo or east along the south shore. Either way it is something only an ocean-touring kayak and an experienced paddler should undertake. Park rangers recommend that open canoes never venture into Lake Superior.

Few if any boats ever find their way into Feldtmann Lake. Nor is the number of hikers who venture to the isolated lake in the southwest corner of the park anywhere near the number of those who visit Lake Richie. The result, for anglers, is superb pike fishing.

Lake Halloran, located off the Feldtmann Ridge Trail and 2.0 miles west of Siskiwit Bay Campground, is even more isolated. The NPS stopped maintaining the side trail to the lake years ago. The signpost is gone and the junction is hidden by a fallen birch tree, but the old trail is still there.

The lake is well known among rangers and trail crews stationed in the Siskiwit Bay area. They know that any trip to Halloran results in some of the largest pike caught on the island.

No matter what lake you venture to or how you choose to reach it, there are advantages to fishing inland. The best is cost. It is far cheaper to hike than to run a cabin cruiser when searching for where the fish are. A fishing license is not needed for the inland lakes—only for Lake Superior, which falls under the jurisdiction of the State of Michigan.

But for many, the best reason is the catch. Hiking in or portaging a boat overland sparks the appetite and heightens the fishing aventure. When the effort is rewarded with a freshly caught pike or trout, dinner is more than a meal. It's a fish story told over and over again.

The Voyageur *(left) and* Wenonah *arrive at Windigo. (Photo by Steve and Carol Maass)*

4   GETTING TO AND AROUND THE ISLAND

The big blue nose of the NPS boat *Ranger III* nudged away from the dock in Houghton, Michigan for its 6½-hour trip to Isle Royale. The passengers were excited. They scrambled on deck to watch the center span of the Houghton–Hancock Bridge raise straight up. They strained to view the nearby shores of the Keweenaw Waterway, a part natural, part man-made canal across the Keweenaw Peninsula.

But when *Ranger III* reached the open waters of Lake Superior, the lively excitement suddenly became quiet contemplation. All on board will meet the "Lady," as the lake is known, and get to know her well before they reach the park. Except for the seagulls or an occasional passing freighter, all there is to view for the next few hours is the lake itself.

She puts backpackers and park visitors in awe. They stand next to the railing and study the world's largest body of fresh water. Her large waves, like fingers from the sea, surge past the boat. The passengers cannot help but feel the power, coldness, and overwhelming size of Lake Superior.

There are two ways to arrive at the Island—by air or by water. You can jump on a small float plane in Houghton and be at the park in 30 minutes. Quick, easy, and not that costly.

But there is something special about making the crossing by boat. By experiencing Lake Superior first, you later gain a sense of Isle Royale's solitude and isolation. The Lady awakens you to the wilderness that she has preserved through time—a wilderness she has protected from man's destructive hands.

You never gain a feeling for the lake by flying over it. And when you land, you arrive at just another national park. Lake Superior is Isle Royale; it surrounds the Island, protects it, gives it the mystic charm that has always lured men and animals across to it.

GETTING THERE

Although *Ranger III* is the most well-known vessel that travels to the Island, several others make the trip from different departure points. Water transportation is available from Houghton and Copper Harbor, Michigan and Grand Portage, Minnesota, the closest of the three.

Ranger III is a government-operated ship that measures 165 feet and carries 123 passengers and pleasure boats up to 20 feet in length. It is the largest vessel operating between Isle Royale and the mainland, and rarely do rough seas prevent her from making the trip. On board is a snack bar, viewing lounges, and a NPS ranger who sells park publications, conducts interpretation programs, helps backpackers with trip plans, and fills out back-country permits for hikers eager to start their wilderness experience the minute they arrive.

Ranger III begins its season in early June and finishes in early September. Operating days and dates vary slightly from year to year for all vessels. *Ranger III* departs Houghton about 9 A.M. from the dock in front of the NPS headquarters and arrives at Rock Harbor Lodge around 3 P.M. It overnights at Rock Harbor before returning to Houghton the following day.

It is wise to get reservations on *Ranger III* or any of the ships. For the NPS boat, reservations can be made starting March 15, Monday through Friday during normal office hours at the park headquarters. Full fare must be paid in advance.

For more information concerning *Ranger III* or to make reservations, contact

Isle Royale National Park
87 N. Ripley St.
Houghton, MI 49931
(906) 482-3310

By traveling northeast along the Keweenaw Peninsula, you can cut the sailing time by 1½ hours. From Copper Harbor at the very tip of the peninsula, the 65-foot *Isle Royale Queen* departs for a 4½-hour trip to the park.

The privately owned ship, which carries 57 passengers, begins its season around mid-May and completes its last trip in mid-September. From about May 14 through June 11 it leaves Copper Harbor Monday through Friday at 8 A.M. for Rock Harbor Lodge. Once arriving at the park the boat turns around, and at 2 P.M. the same day returns to Copper Harbor. From mid-June to early September the vessel leaves Copper Harbor Monday through Saturday at 8 A.M. and departs Rock Harbor the same day at 3:30 P.M. From about September 10 through September 27 it returns to its early-season schedule. Consult the park's latest transportation brochure for current schedule.

There is no food service on board, and full deposit is required. Once again, reservations are strongly recommended and can be made year 'round. For more information or to make reservations contact

> Isle Royale Ferry Service
> Copper Harbor, MI 49918
> (906) 482-4950 (winter)
> (906) 289-4437 (summer)

Two privately owned ferries depart from Grand Portage for the 2½-hour trip to the park. Both stop at Windigo, the ranger station at the western end of the Island.

The 64-foot *Wenonah,* which carries 150 passengers, runs from mid-June to early September. The ship departs daily from Grand Portage at 9:30 A.M. and then returns from Windigo the same day at 3 P.M.

The other vessel out of Grand Portage is the 60-foot *Voyageur,* which carries 49 passengers. The boat is piloted by Roy Oberg, an old-timer who has been associated with Isle Royale long before it was a national park. Roy not only gets you to the Island, but enlightens you with tidbits of its colorful history.

Voyageur runs from about May 12 through October 23. From about May 12 to May 30 it departs Grand Portage Wednesday and Saturday at 9:30 A.M., stops at Windigo, and overnights at Rock Harbor Lodge. The following day, either Thursday or Sunday, it departs from Rock Harbor at 8 A.M. for Windigo and Grand Portage.

The schedule is the same from early June to early September, except *Voyageur* includes a third trip that departs from Grand Portage on Monday with a return from Rock Harbor Lodge on Tuesday. From about September 15 to October 23, *Voyageur* returns to its early-season schedule.

Reservations for *Wenonah* and *Voyageur* are taken year 'round, and full deposit is required. To make reservations or obtain information on both vessels, contact

> GPIR Transportation Line, Inc.
> 1332 London Rd.
> Duluth MI 55805
> (218) 728-1237

Regularly scheduled seaplane service is available out of Houghton either for Windigo or Rock Harbor Lodge. Many backpackers take advantage of the service by taking the plane to Windigo, hiking to Rock Harbor Lodge, and returning on *Ranger III.*

Sky Ranger, a 9-passenger floatplane, makes the trip from about June 12 through Labor Day, with daily flights that depart at 8 A.M. for Windigo and at 10 A.M. for Rock Harbor Lodge. The plane returns from Windigo daily at about 8:30 A.M. and from Rock Harbor at 3 P.M. *Dornier*, a 6-passenger floatplane, fills in from about May 22 through June 11 and September 7 through September 25, with a daily flight to Rock Harbor Lodge at noon, returning to Houghton at 1 P.M. *Dornier* can also be chartered any time during the season.

Backpackers are allowed 35 pounds of gear with each fare. A reservation can be secured with a deposit of 25 percent of the full fare. For reservations or more information contact

Isle Royale Seaplane Service

June–August	September–May
P.O. Box 371	248 Airport Rd.
Houghton, MI 49931	Shawano, WI 54166
(906) 482-8850	(715) 526-2465

It is important to remember the extra transportation costs when planning a trip to Isle Royale.

GETTING AROUND

Backpackers on a tight time schedule often find it necessary to use intra-island transportation to complete their trip or to meet ferry connections for their return home.

After arriving at Windigo, *Voyageur* circumnavigates the Island clockwise and can be used to hop from one section of the park to another. Canoeists and kayakers can also use the ship to skip open stretches of Lake Superior. From Windigo, the vessel stops at McCargoe Cove Campground, Belle Isle Campground, and then overnights at Rock Harbor Lodge. The following day it continues with stops at Daisy Farm, Chippewa Harbor Campground, Malone Bay Campground, and Windigo before returning to Grand Portage. You should make arrangements with the captain if you wish to be picked up at locations other than Rock Harbor and Windigo.

The park also has a water-taxi service that will drop off backpackers and campers at different spots in Rock Harbor, including Tookers Island Campground, Three-Mile Campground, Daisy Farm, or Moskey Basin. This avoids the stampede that results when *Ranger III* arrives and 50 to 70 hikers rush down the trail. Once you arrive, inquire at the Rock Harbor store or visitor center for more details.

5 ENJOYING THE BACK COUNTRY

A twig broke.

The noise pierced the air, and I instinctively froze. At first there was only a stillness in the trees. But when I stepped lightly off the Greenstone Ridge Trail, two bull moose broke out of a clump of spruce and galloped 50 yards south. Seeing a moose is always a joy on the Island. Seeing two bulls is a rare treat. For five minutes we stood and stared at each other. Though bulls shy away from humans most of the summer, the tender young aspen trees were too tempting. They resumed eating.

With my camera in hand, I slowly began to reduce the gap between us. The second bull moved out of my sight, but the big one was straight in front of me, less than 50 yards away. Every well-placed step made him a little larger in my viewfinder. My heart was throbbing, my shutter finger was busy—45 yards, *click*; 42 yards, *click*; 40 yards, *click*; 35 yards, *click*.

Suddenly, there was a large crash to my right, and I gasped as the second bull stepped out of a grove of trees and looked me dead in the pupils from less than 15 yards away. My heart stopped, but my shutter finger instinctively went to work.

Click.

There was no language barrier between us. We both understood each other well, and I began to retreat. On the third step, my foot caught a log, and I ended up sitting in a pile of last winter's moose nuggets. Both bulls looked at me and casually strolled off. Something that can't walk, can't be too dangerous.

SEEING THE BACK COUNTRY

There are three requirements for escaping beyond Rock Harbor Lodge and Windigo. Hiking and paddling demand some outdoor experience, good equipment, and a little grunting as you make your way around the Island. Camping requires experience and equipment but significantly reduces the need for a strong—and willing—back to carry a pack or boat.

By using intrapark water transportation (see Chapter 4) you could circle the park and stay at shoreline campgrounds without ever having to haul your gear any farther than from the dock to the first available shelter or campsite. Day hikes with light packs will allow you to view most of the park easily.

These day hikers are usually well equipped, with little or no weight limit on gear. These backpackers must plan ahead—and carefully. Campgrounds have user's limits that range from one to three days, and water transportation is not a daily service in most areas of the park. Camp-

Back country camp. (Photo by Steve and Carol Maass)

grounds that have transportation either from Rock Harbor Lodge or Windigo are McCargoe Cove, Belle Isle, Tooker's Island, Three-Mile, Daisy Farm, Moskey Basin, Chippewa Harbor, and Malone Bay.

Most shoreline campgrounds—those on the coast of Lake Superior—have shelters. The floors are harder to sleep on than the ground, but they are roomier and drier than most tents. Even outdoor purists use them occasionally, because they are a great place to sort and dry out gear before tackling another section of the trail.

Never count on getting a shelter. Always have a tent with you. Shelters are available on a first-come-first-serve basis, and at many popular campgrounds they are taken by early afternoon.

Because of the limitations of water transportation, hiking is by far a more popular—and cheaper—way to see the back country. The park trails are well marked and easy to follow, with the exception of the rugged Minong Ridge route. You don't have to be a seasoned outdoorsman to hike Isle Royale. Day hikers will find the park ideal for their first week-long expedition.

But you do have to be in shape and arrive with the proper equipment. For those who are not and who lack the necessary equipment, the Island can be and is a dangerous place. There are no alpine trails in the park, but there are ridges—and the constant up-and-down trek over them is almost as tiring as hiking in the mountains.

The park has no medical services beyond what rangers can provide with their first-aid kits. A seriously sick or injured person possibly could be stranded for a day or two before help arrives.

Hikers can put together several trail combinations for a week-long tramp. Most first-time visitors tackle the Greenstone Ridge Trail, or the "Boulevard" as it is known to some trail crews. The trail runs along nearly the entire length of the ridge, from Lookout Louise to Windigo. Backpackers usually skip the first part and hike just the 42 miles from Rock Harbor Lodge to the Island's western end in 4 or 5 days. That leaves the final 2 days of their week's vacation for traveling to and from the park.

The Greenstone Ridge Trail receives the greatest amount of traffic during July and August. Backpackers who wish to avoid much of that can arrive at Windigo and hike the Feldtmann Ridge, Island Mine, the first leg of the Greenstone, and the Huginnin Cove trails for a 5-day circular route. This would include nights spent at Feldtmann Lake, Siskiwit Bay, Island Mine, and Huginnin Cove—scenic campgrounds that are not as busy as those along the Greenstone.

All trails and campgrounds along Rock Harbor are busy during July and August, but by taking a boat to Malone Bay Campground you can escape much of it. From here you could hike Ishpeming Trail, part of the Greenstone to Hatchet Lake, cut across north to the Minong Ridge Trail, and then return to Rock Harbor through the beautiful inland lakes. On this route, nights can be spent at several pleasant campgrounds, including Malone Bay, Todd Harbor, and McCargoe Cove.

For those with backpacking experience who want to avoid people as much as possible, Minong Ridge Trail is the route to choose. Much of it is unplanked and not very well marked, making it a challenge to any hiker. Most of it follows a knee-bending, up-and-down pattern along the bare rocky ridge from McCargoe Cove nearly to Windigo.

The Minong is a hard, boot-soaking hike, but it rewards backpackers with plenty of wildlife and beautiful views of the Island and Lake Superior. If you plan to go from Rock Harbor Lodge to Windigo, or the other way around, plan on 6 or 7 days. And if you normally cover a mile with a full pack on in 20 or 30 minutes, plan on some parts of the trail taking you 45 minutes to more than an hour to walk a mile.

For those unsure where they want to hike, read the rest of this guide and then plan your own route. Keep in mind the following grades used in this book to judge the difficulty of trails:

Easy: An easy-to-follow, relatively level trail that can almost be done in tennis shoes. An average hiker can cover a mile in 20 or 30 minutes.

Moderate: Most of the trails fall into this category. There is some climbing over ridges, but the path is well marked and planked. Average hikers can plan on a 30–45-minute hike.

Difficult: A poorly marked trail or one that has a considerable amount of climbing. A mile will take 40 minutes to well over an hour on some parts of the Minong.

The third way to see the backcountry is by paddling. For those who have the equipment and experience, this is the best method of them all. You work less, see more, and are able to isolate yourself in the park, something that is very difficult for campers or hikers to do.

Most paddlers arrive with a canoe, which is adequate. **But remember that park officials strongly recommend that canoeists stay out of the open waters of Lake Superior.** Open canoes are too unprotected and unstable for most paddlers to handle the large waves or sudden squalls the lake can kick up.

The alternative to canoeing is kayaking. Although kayaks are seen only a few times each summer, they also are a good way to go. The boat is more stable in rough water and can venture in such areas as Siskiwit Bay or around the southwest shore of the park where canoeists are discouraged from going. Still, kayakers too should be experienced in the use of their craft.

Either way, the price you have to pay for the easy paddling is portaging your boat and carrying your equipment and food on a second trip. There is no easy way to get around portaging. Some portages are a 75-yard hop, skip, and jump like the Pickerel Cove portage. The one to Lake Richie is a two-mile grunt.

This book divides the park into four areas as far as paddling is concerned. A week-long canoe trip would mean traveling through two areas with at least one or two portages each day. The four areas are as follows.

The Five Fingers: This area at the east end of the park consists of long fiord-like bays, coves, and harbors. It is one of the more beautiful areas to paddle and a personal favorite of many. Although a strong paddler could go from McCargoe Cove to Rock Harbor in a day, you could spend a week exploring each island and cove in the area.

Northern Inland Lakes: These consist of Lake Richie, Lake LeSage, Lake Livermore, Chickenbone Lake, and McCargoe Cove. It is part of a common route where canoers paddle from Rock Harbor to McCargoe Cove and then cut through the Five Fingers back to Rock Harbor Lodge.

Southern Inland Lakes: This area is not as heavily used, and it is here where paddlers can find solitude. The waterways consist of Chippewa Harbor, Lake Whittlesey, Wood Lake, Siskiwit Lake, and Intermediate Lake. The fishing is superb, and anglers will be rewarded with plenty of pike and, possibly, walleye and lake trout. Along with the popular and scenic Malone Bay and Chippewa Harbor campgrounds, there are four canoe campgrounds reached only by paddlers. The Wood Lake Campground is one of the most beautiful and isolated in the park.

South Shore: It is possible for experienced kayakers with the proper storm gear and enough time to paddle Lake Superior's south shore. The route runs from Malone Bay Campground through Siskiwit Bay and into the open waters of Lake Superior to Windigo, at the end of Washington

Harbor. Kayakers will be in open water for much of the way, but the south shore offers more beaches and coves than its northern counterpart for emergency landings in case of rough conditions. Not even kayakers should attempt the north shore from Washington Harbor to McCargoe Cove, because the coastline consists of sharp cliffs with few if any places to land.

Before anybody considers paddling the Island, they should be aware of the danger involved in tipping over in Lake Superior. The water, even in the summer, is never more than a few degrees above freezing. Five minutes in Lake Superior and you would be unable to move your fingers. Ten minutes and you would lose control of your legs and arms. Thirty minutes in the lake and you would die of exposure.

The Lady is famous for suddenly turning calm waters into rough seas with high winds or a squall. Canoeists, and especially kayakers, considering the south shore, should always plan extra days in case they are forced to sit out stormy weather. Never take a chance in questionable weather just to make the ferry back to the mainland.

PERMITS

The final way of seeing the Island is cross-country travel through the trail-less areas of the park. This adventure is strictly for highly experienced backpackers, because it is a very difficult form of travel. Ponds and bogs are scattered throughout Isle Royale, and the Island's north-facing slopes are steep, with some cliffs exceeding 100 feet in height.

Persons interested in cross-country travel must plan far ahead with park officials and obtain a back country permit and list their itinerary. Kayakers considering the south shore also need the permit, because there are no campgrounds on this section of shoreline. Certain zones are closed to camping each summer to protect sensitive wildlife habitat.

Other hikers and paddlers also need a back-country permit. This permit can be obtained free of charge at the visitor center at Windigo or Rock Harbor when you arrive or on board *Ranger III* on the way to the Island.

BACK-COUNTRY NEEDS

Prepare for Isle Royale as you would for any wilderness area. Come with the right equipment, but don't arrive with too much. For a 1-week trip, the backpack should not exceed $\frac{1}{5}$ of your body weight. No one should be lugging around a 45- or 50-pound pack.

Boots: Tennis shoes alone won't do. You need good, sturdy, hiking boots, broken in before you land at Rock Harbor Lodge. The boots should be heavily waxed to combat all the moisture and rain you will most likely

Paddling through the Five Fingers area islets. (Photo by Steve and Carol Maass)

run into. Foot gear should include wool socks and moleskin; and keep some bandages ready to be applied at the first sign of tenderness.

Tent: Even when it rains, you don't spend much time in your tent, so a light-weight nylon unit that weighs from 6 to 8 pounds is sufficient. It should have a rain fly and bug-proof netting. Also take a ground cloth and sleeping pad.

Stove: Opportunities for campfires are very limited, and even if you can build them, much of the wood on the Island is wet or of poor cook-fire quality. A small, self-contained backpacker stove is a must. You'll be thankful you have it when it rains. White gas is available at the Rock Harbor Lodge and Windigo stores.

Clothes: Come prepared for cool, wet weather—then when the sun breaks out, you won't mind lugging around the extra clothes. In every backpack should be a wool hat and mittens, a heavy jersey or coat, and rain gear (pants and jacket). Bring a pair of walking shorts In warm weather.

Insect repellent: Bugs are a part of any wilderness area, and Isle Royale is no exception. From June through mid-August you will be greeted by mosquitoes, black flies, and gnats. Some places are worse than others. Keep your bug dope within easy reach.

Maps: Every hiking party should have a map and compass *and* somebody who knows how to use them together. The best map is the U.S. Geological Survey topographic map of Isle Royale, which has a scale of 1:62,500. It can be purchased at Windigo, Rock Harbor Lodge, Houghton, or by mail.

Canoeing equipment: The easiest way to portage a boat is for one person to balance it on his or her shoulders and carry it lengthwise. The easiest way to do that is with a portage yoke that straps to the sides of the boat. Bring waterproof bags for all gear, especially your sleeping bag, camera, and food. An extra paddle and a repair kit of duct tape and a few tools are also reassuring.

WEATHER

Lake Superior has a great modifying effect on the Island. It keeps the winters milder and the summers cooler than those experienced 20 miles away on the mainland. Daytime temperatures range from 60 to 70 °F most of the summer and occasionally will exceed 80 °F in mid-August. The nights are cool and in early or late summer can easily drop below 40 °F.

Thunderstorms and rain showers are common throughout the summer, and dense fog appears frequently in the spring and early summer.

That brings us to the question of what is the best time to visit the park. It all depends on your likes and dislikes. If you can't stand bugs, you will want to arrive mid-August or early September. If you are crazy about wildflowers, mid-June to early July is the best time. Fishermen prefer June, and many backpackers arrive mid-to-late September to catch the spectacular fall colors.

The park is officially open from May through October, and generally the best weather—sunshine and warm temperatures—occurs from mid-July to mid-August. But that is only a general rule. The Island is full of exceptions from year to year, and the weather is always one of them. It is best to prepare for anything.

BACK-COUNTRY WATER

Although no one seems to know the last reported case of a visitor getting tapeworm, park rangers consider all water on and around Isle Royale to be contaminated with the eggs of the parasite. Only the water from the spigots at Rock Harbor Lodge, Windigo, and Daisy Farm is safe to drink without treating.

The tapeworm lives in a cycle that goes from the scat of the wolf to the water and then into the moose when the animal eats aquatic vegetation. The cycle is completed when wolves kill the moose and consume the eggs unknowingly.

It is important to realize that bringing water just to a boil or using iodine or purification tablets will not destroy the eggs. Water must be boiled for at least two minutes before the eggs are killed.

An easier alternative is to use a water filter. The filter has to have a screen that will trap particles 25 microns or smaller. Both camp stores usually have filters for sale, but it is cheaper if you buy one before arriving. Contact the park for an updated list of recommended filters.

One-quart filters clean more water at a time but are usually bulky to haul around. The 6-ounce filters are the best if you are traveling with someone else. Use a coffee filter first before using your water purifier on the silty water found in bogs.

WHAT'S AVAILABLE ON THE ISLAND?

You could almost outfit an expedition at the Rock Harbor store. The small store across from the visitor center has many items, ranging from freeze-dried dinners and trail munch to fishing tackle, pots, and day packs. However, don't plan to stock your trip here. The quantities are limited and often run out until the next boat arrives from Houghton. Also, the prices are higher than on the mainland.

The camp store doesn't really cater to newly arrived hikers so much as to those just coming off the trail. Weary backpackers find an incredible selection of sweets to satisfy their junk-food depletion or sugar craving.

Those ending their trek at Rock Harbor have several ways of easing themselves back into civilization. A shower, clean towel, and a bar of soap can be obtained at the camp store. After six days of freeze-dried chicken a la king, you might want to take in a dinner at the lodge dining room. Dinners are expensive but worth it.

Some backpackers even like to book a room for their final night at Rock Harbor, either at the lodge or in one of the housekeeping units that can be shared by six people and feature small kitchenettes. Reservations are strongly recommended, but visitors can occasionally get last-minute accommodations because of cancellations. For reservations contact the headquarters of the park concessionaire, located in Kentucky:

National Park Concessions, Inc.
Mammoth Cave, KY 42259
(502) 773-2191

Canoes are also available at Rock Harbor and Windigo for paddling in the local area. The rates are based on a half- or full-day rental and include paddles and life jackets. At Rock Harbor Lodge you can also rent a rowboat and 9½-hp motor. Inquire at the camp stores about rentals.

Back country snooze. (Photo by Steve and Carol Maass)

MORE INFORMATION

The Isle Royale Natural History Association is a nonprofit organization that publishes and sells a variety of inexpensive books and pamphlets about the park. Many cover the colorful history of the Island, and others look into the special wolf–moose relationship. There are also many field guides that help backpackers understand and enjoy the wilderness they travel through.

The following are a few of the booklets that might interest hikers and canoeists:

Fishes of Isle Royale by K. F. Lagler and C. R. Goldman. General guide to sport fishing for the park.

101 Wildflowers of Isle Royale by Robert A. Janke. Drawings and descriptions of common wildflowers found on the Island.

Wildlife of Isle Royale by P. Jordan and O. Shelton. Checklists and information on the park's birds, mammals, amphibians, reptiles, and fishes.

The Life of Isle Royale by Napier Shelton. Complete natural history of the park, with color illustrations and animal checklists.

The books are on sale at Rock Harbor Lodge and Windigo visitor centers, on board *Ranger III,* and at the park headquarters at Houghton. You can also order them ahead of time or receive a complete publications list by writing to:

>Isle Royale Natural History Association
>87 N. Ripley St.
>Houghton, MI 49931

LOW-IMPACT CAMPING

The only way the NPS can preserve the Island for future use and still allow the 15,000 visitors to arrive every summer is to practice "low-impact use." The park is fragile, and careless use will disturb its wildlife, delicate plants, and thin layer of soil.

Thus, visitors—hikers and canoeists, especially—must reduce their impact on the land. The Island as we know it will survive only if we are careful how we treat it. On the back of every backcountry use-permit are these rules:

• Fires are permitted only in grills and metal rings. Use dead and down wood. Do not peel bark or cut live trees.

• Cross-country campers must use backpacking stoves. No wood fires allowed.

• All trash must be carried out and not burned or buried.

• Pitch tents only in designated sites as marked in each campground. Do not clear brush away to set up a tent.

• Groups must camp only in group sites.

• Do not wash or throw wastewater into or close to any water source, stream or lake.

• When you break camp, leave no trace.

And please: no radios or tape recorders while visiting the park. The solitude of nature is too rare and valuable to disturb with man-made music.

Indian Portage Trail. (Photo by Steve and Carol Maass)

PART TWO

ISLE ROYALE ON FOOT

6 THE BOULEVARD

GREENSTONE RIDGE TRAIL

Distance: 40 miles
Hiking time: 4–5 days
High point: 1394 feet
Rating: moderate

The Island is a maze of footpaths, but it is the longer trails, the ones that reach far into the back country, that seem to give hikers their best memories. These pathways lead away from crowded campgrounds and busy shorelines to the solitude that is Isle Royale.

Of the handful of trails that stretch across the park, only the Greenstone Ridge Trail could be called the "Boulevard." It is the most popular, best marked, and longest trail on Isle Royale. It runs along the backbone of the park, stretching from Windigo to Lookout Louise, near the northeast end.

Although the trail is rated moderate, there is an occasional difficult section with a knee-bending climb. Experienced hikers in good shape can cover the 40-plus miles in 3 days. But the Greenstone can also be a good trail for beginners if they come with light packs and have 4 or 5 days to walk it.

It is debatable which is easier: starting at Rock Harbor Lodge or Windigo. The steeper grades are encountered just outside of Windigo, and many hikers prefer to get them over with the first day. Others like to begin at Rock Harbor and have the rapid walk down Sugar Mountain for the final leg.

But for most hikers, transportation arrangements determine where they start. Because the majority of visitors arrive at Rock Harbor, this guide describes the trail from east to west, beginning at Lookout Louise junction.

Only a backpacking fanatic, who wants to hike every last inch of the Boulevard, would arrange to be taken by boat from Rock Harbor across Tobin Harbor to the Lookout Louise Trail, which begins at Hidden Lake. Most hikers either walk the Tobin Harbor or Rock Harbor trails and spend their first night at Three Mile Campground. The following day they take the Mount Franklin Trail to the Greenstone (see page 96, maps on pages 95 and 97).

Rock Harbor Lodge

Before jumping on the trail, backpackers have to pass by Rock Harbor Lodge. The visitor center and camp store are immediately in front of you after you disembark from the boat. Backpackers who did not pick up a back-country use permit from the NPS ranger on *Ranger III*, should do so at the visitor center.

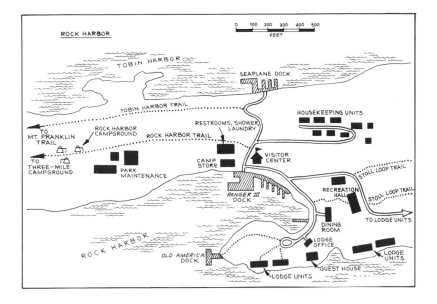

The Rock Harbor Lodge area—which includes the hotel, house-keeping cabins, quarters for concession and NPS workers, and a public campground—can be a busy place with visitors arriving and departing at the same time. Some hikers prefer to pick up their permits and maps and then depart the same day to spend their first night at Three-Mile Campground.

But most spend their first night in Rock Harbor Campground, which has nine shelters, group and individual campsites, piped-in water, tables, garbage cans, and pit toilets. It is wise to stake out a shelter or a tent site as soon as you arrive: the campground can fill quickly during the height of the summer. There is a one-night limit in the Rock Harbor Campground.

Lookout Louise to Mount Franklin

Distance: 4.8 miles

The Greenstone Ridge Trail begins at the junction with the Lookout Louise Trail. From the sign-posted junction, Lookout Louise lies 0.1 miles to the north, Tobin Harbor 0.9 miles to the south, and Windigo 40 miles (not including spurs to campgrounds), at the west end of the Greenstone Trail.

The Greenstone departs from the Lookout Louise Trail and winds through an open ridgetop for 0.5 miles until it arrives at an exhibit on the ancient copper pits. Indians pounded out the pits 3000 years ago to obtain pure copper. Several pits are located near the display.

The trail continues along the open ridge and quickly becomes one of the most pleasant walks on the Island. Most of the hike is level and gives way

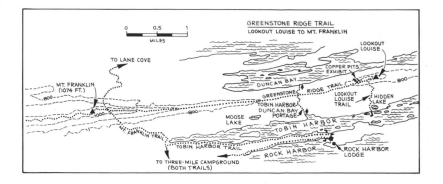

to occasional views of Tobin Harbor to the south and Duncan Bay to the north. The only problem is the thick brush—thimbleberry, especially—that develops from mid-to-late summer. At times it completely covers the path. Backpackers who hike with their heads to the ground might discover a small strawberry patch here and there.

After 1.4 miles from the beginning, the trail arrives at the junction of the canoe portage from Duncan Bay to Tobin Harbor. Although the portage is only 0.8 miles, it is the most difficult because it climbs 175 feet in an extremely steep fashion.

The ridgetop remains exposed for another mile or so and then gradually becomes sparsely wooded, with only a rare glimpse of the harbors from the trail. Moose sign—prints, droppings, and stripped aspen trees—are plentiful in this area, as are the animals themselves.

Just before reaching the top of Mount Franklin, the trail arrives at the junction with the trail to Lane Cove. This pretty little cove and campground lie 2.3 miles to the northwest, and Three-Mile Campground is 2.2 miles to the south, at the end of the Mount Franklin Trail.

The Greenstone climbs gently for 0.3 miles until it reaches the top of Mount Franklin (1074 feet), a spot marked by large rocks. Here, backpackers sit and admire the excellent view of the northeastern end of the park, the outlying islands, and the Canadian shoreline. The mountain was named after Benjamin Franklin (see Chapter 1).

Mount Franklin to West Chickenbone Campground

Distance: 10.0 miles

From the peak of Mount Franklin, the trail descends sharply into a sparsely wooded area. Here, the trail levels out for 0.25 miles before climbing gently back up to the open, rocky ridge top. Hikers again are rewarded with views on the final 2.0 miles to Mount Ojibway along a fairly level path.

A word of caution: The open sections of the ridge can become

Autumn on the Greenstone Ridge Trail. (Photo by Steve and Carol Maass)

overgrown with brush that will leave you soaking wet after a rain storm. In places the trail might also become difficult to see in the brush.

The trail continues along the rocky crest of the ridge for almost 2.0 miles until it reaches Mount Ojibway (1136 feet), marked by a park service lookout tower. At the tower is the junction with the Mount Ojibway Trail. This is the first of two trails heading south for Daisy Farm Campground, which lies 1.5 miles to the south on Rock Harbor.

The Greenstone departs from the Ojibway Lookout Tower and descends west into wooded terrain. In 1.5 miles the trail climbs gently and reaches the junction of the Daisy Farm Trail—the second trail to Daisy Farm Campground, 1.9 miles to the southeast.

From the junction, the Greenstone goes over several small knolls and then descends toward Angleworm Lake. At one point the trail comes within ⅛ mile of the lake, although thick forest keeps the body of water hidden most of the summer. There is no maintained side trail to Angleworm Lake, but fishermen who want to wet their lines can easily bushwhack it to the shore of this fine northern pike fishing spot.

The pathway begins another climb, where it reaches a high point of 934 feet and then descends again to dense forest with scattered bogs. The trail remains in this terrain for a spell before making a gradual ascent to an open crest on the ridge. Here, the birch trees thin out for more than 1.0 miles.

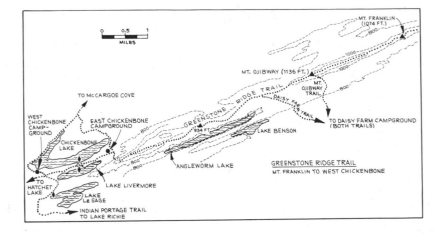

The level walk ends near a rock overhang from which you can view the north side of the Island, Pie Island in Ontario, and the east end of Chickenbone Lake. The trail departs from the picturesque spot, descends a little, and then makes a 90°-turn. From here it drops quickly off the Greenstone Ridge and into a bog before reaching the junction with the East Chickenbone Trail, which heads 2.1 miles northwest to McCargoe Cove.

Just 300 feet north of the Greenstone is East Chickenbone Campground, located on a ridge above the east shore of the lake. The campground has individual and group campsites and pit toilets. It is located partially in the trees.

The Greenstone Ridge Trail resumes west from the junction with the East Chickenbone Trail and follows the thin strip of land separating Chickenbone Lake to the north and Lake Livermore to the south. Occasionally through the trees you can catch views of both bodies of water. After about 1.0 miles, the trail arrives at the short portage between the two lakes and then dips down to cross a stream. From here it continues for another mile of easy walking until it reaches one of the park's major trail junctions.

This is where the Indian Portage Trail and the Greenstone cross. To the south on the Indian Portage Trail lies Lake Richie (3.4 miles) and Chippewa Harbor (7.8 miles) campgrounds; McCargoe Cove is 2.9 miles to the north. From this point, Hatchet Lake Campground is 7.7 miles to the west along the Greenstone, and Windigo is 25.8 miles.

The West Chickenbone Campground is 0.2 miles north of the Greenstone Ridge Trail and is a favorite among backpackers. A pretty area situated on the shores of the lake, the campground has individual and group campsites and pit toilets. The lake itself is excellent for pike and yellow perch and an occasional walleye. Beaver lodges dot the far shore, and moose frequent the waters.

West Chickenbone Campground to Hatchet Lake Campground

Distance: 7.8 miles

Backtrack to the junction of the Indian Portage and Greenstone Ridge Trails, and from here the Greenstone climbs up and over a low hill and then levels out 0.5 miles through thick forest. After crossing a planked stream, the trail begins its first steep climb to Hatchet Lake.

The climb is a backbreaker, especially with a pack on, but once you reach the top of the first knoll you are rewarded with perhaps the best view of the inland lakes. Before you to the east is McCargoe Cove, followed by Chickenbone, Livermore, and LeSage lakes. To the south, you can spot Intermediate Lake, Lake Siskiwit, and Siskiwit Bay.

From here the trail winds through somewhat open terrain for a short spell before ascending near the rocky crest of the Greenstone. By scrambling over loose rocks to the top of the ridge, you can get more views of the inland lakes. The trail, meanwhile, dips back into scattered forest and then climbs another high point. Then the trail drops once more into forest before making its final assault up Mount Siskiwit (1205 feet). The trail doesn't really reach the peak but passes nearby.

The trail drops sharply off Mount Siskiwit and levels out for a short spell along the ridge, where you can view both sides of the Island. The path continues to descend in sharp spurts and eventually arrives at a bog with a planked stream that has little or no water during dry spells.

After crossing the bog, the trail rises sharply with the ridge and then levels out with an occasional dip and climb for the next 1.5 miles. The forest has a few rocky clearings, and caution has to be used not to lose the trail in these spots. Eventually, the trail makes one last short climb and reaches the junction of the trail to Hatchet Lake Campground.

This side trail—the Hatchet Lake Trail—connects the Greenstone with the Minong Ridge Trail, 2.6 miles to the north after passing the lakeside

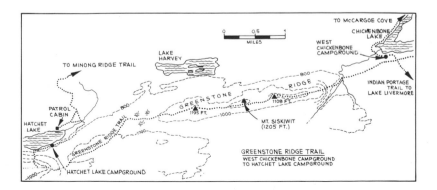

campground. Ishpeming Lookout Tower lies 3.8 miles further west on the Greenstone, and the junction with the trail to West Chickenbone Campground is 7.2 miles to the east.

After spending a day climbing over Mount Siskiwit, you may not find Hatchet Lake Campground the most pleasant spot to rest. The campground has been moved and is now 0.5 miles from the junction of the Greenstone Ridge Trail. That in itself dismays many backpackers who expect to just run down to the lake and find a campsite as shown on the older maps. The campsite is now further along the side trail to the Minong Ridge and is situated in the woods. Hatchet Lake has pit toilets, group and individual campsites, and can get buggy at times. Unfortunately, it's a long hike to the next campground.

Hatchet Lake Campground
to South Lake Desor Campground

Distance: 8.2 miles

The Greenstone Ridge Trail departs from the Hatchet Lake junction and climbs sharply for about 50 yards to a rocky crest. The view of Siskiwit Lake is fine, but it is only one of many in the next 1.5-mile stretch. The footpath dips up and down between stands of birch and open patches of the ridge, where at times you can see nearly the entire lake to the south. Be careful over the rocky areas: You can easily lose the trail.

About 1.5 miles from the junction, the trail climbs steeply and then levels off for a short spell. Keep an eye out for an unmarked side trail to the right that leads off a short distance to clearings with incredible views of Hatchet Lake, Todd Harbor, and Lake Superior. The trail descends again, levels off through birch forests and then sharply climbs to another high point with more side paths to viewing points.

From here the trail winds through open clearings without too much dipping for 0.5 miles before it makes another noticeable descent. The trail

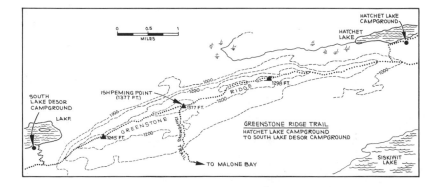

Hatchet Lake from Greenstone Ridge.

levels off for a short distance and begins its final 0.5-mile climb to Ishpeming Point (1377 feet), the second highest point in the park.

The climb can be a knee-bender, and, unfortunately, Ishpeming Point is a rather disappointing place because views are blocked by trees. But there is a lookout tower here, even if it is rather low to the ground, and nearby the junction with the side trail to Malone Bay Campground.

The Ishpeming Trail departs from here and heads south 7.6 miles to Malone Bay. The tower is almost halfway between Lake Desor (3.9 miles) and Hatchet Lake Campground (4.3 miles) along the Greenstone.

The next 4.0 miles to Lake Desor is completely different from the first four from Hatchet Lake. The walk to Lake Desor seems shorter, has less up-and-down hiking, but provides few views of anything other than the trees next to the path.

The trail departs west from the lookout tower and immediately re-enters forest terrain. It descends gradually with an occasional climb before leveling off for nearly 1.0 miles to cross a small bog.

The final 1.0 miles of the trail gradually descends until it reaches the junction of the trail to South Lake Desor Campground. The campground is 0.4 miles from the junction of the Greenstone Ridge Trail; Island Mine Campground is 5.1 miles further west along the Greenstone.

Although situated above the shoreline and not on it, the South Lake Desor Campground is definitely a step above the campground at Hatchet Lake. The area has individual and group campsites, toilets, and fewer bugs than Hatchet. The lake is supposed to have brook trout in it, but few anglers have much luck in Desor.

South Lake Desor Campground
to Washington Creek Campground

Distance: 11.3 miles

The side trail and South Lake Desor Campground have been moved since the U.S. Geological Survey maps were drawn for Isle Royale. The campground is no longer at the end of the lake but is now 1.0 miles west along the southern shore.

The Greenstone Ridge Trail departs from the junction of the campground trail and immediately makes a steep ascent to the ridge. It climbs over a hump, drops slightly, and then makes another ascent to a high point on the ridge, where there is a clearing in the trees. Enjoy the sun and the quick views of Lake Desor to the east, for such breaks in the foliage are rare on the remainder of the trail.

The trail climbs a second ridge, and you should keep an eye out for an unmarked side trail that leads off to the north. It swings out to another rocky clearing and supplies a superb view of Lake Desor, the Minong Ridge, and across Lake Superior to Canada. The side trail circles back to the Greenstone Ridge Trail.

The trail drops again and then makes its final and steepest climb to the top of Mount Desor (1394 feet), the highest point on the Island. Arriving at the summit is a disappointment, because it is covered with sugar-maple trees and offers no views. Some hikers go right by without ever knowing they have just climbed to the park's lofty perch.

From the mountain the trail descends gradually for more than 1.5 miles, where it levels out and crosses a bog. The NPS trail crew has thoughtfully planked most of the trail to protect the terrain and so backpackers don't have to wander through knee-deep mud.

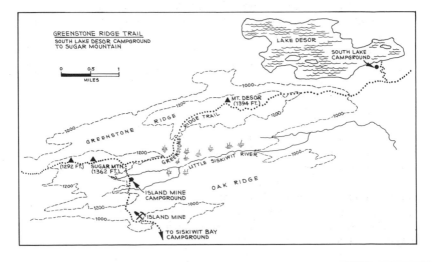

Backpacker on the Greenstone Trail. (Photo by Steve and Carol Maass)

Eventually, the foot path climbs the ridge and arrives at the junction with the Island Mine Trail. To the south, along this side trail, is Island Mine Campground (0.3 miles) and Siskiwit Bay Campground (4.7 miles). Lake Desor lies 5.2 miles to the east at this point, and Washington Creek Campground is 6.1 miles to the west.

The Island Mine Campground is deep in the sugar-maple forest and provides individual and group campsites and pit toilets. Water is available from a nearby stream, which can become sluggish and stagnant during dry spells.

By this time hikers are in good shape and many prefer to push on to Windigo. The Greenstone Ridge Trail departs from the junction of the trail to Island Mine Campground and gradually climbs the remaining distance to the top of Sugar Mountain (1362 feet), the third highest point on the Island.

The mountain is named after the sugar-maple trees that cover it and make up the forest most of the way to Windigo. As late as the 1870s Indians arrived at Sugar Mountain to tap the trees for their sweet sap.

From the peak of Sugar Mountain it is 5.5 miles to Windigo along a trail that is mostly downhill. Mostly, that is. The path dips and climbs the entire way but three times ascends high points in the ridge, followed by a sharp drop. At each drop, hikers eager to reach the final campground and raid the camp store, think they are closing in on their destination only to be disappointed.

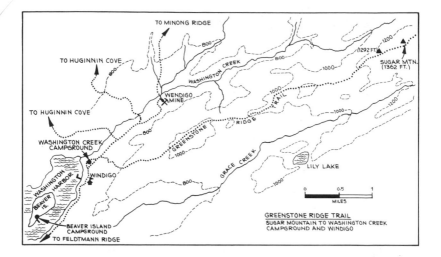

After the third drop, the trail levels out for a short spell before dropping sharply into Washington Creek Basin. Here, it ends at the junction with the Washington Creek Trail. To the west on the trail is Washington Creek Campground (0.3 miles); Minong Ridge Trail begins 1.3 miles to the east. From this point Island Mine Campground is 6.1 miles down the Greenstone Ridge Trail.

After reaching Washington Creek Campground it is a good idea to stake out a shelter or campsite before continuing on. The campground has 10 shelters along the creek, toilets, tables, garbage cans, and piped-in water, along with individual and group campsites. The creek is known for its fine brook-trout fishing, and anglers do well for pike at the mouth of the stream. There is usually a camp moose—if not a couple—who frequent the stream at dusk.

Another 0.25 miles west is Windigo, where there are public showers, laundry and toilets, a small store, a visitor center, and a major boat dock. The center sells park publications, issues back-country permits, and greets visitors. Near the visitor center is a side trail that leads to the amphitheater and store.

If Washington Creek Campground is too crowded for you, one alternative is to rent a canoe at the camp store for a day and paddle out to Beaver Island, a short distance away. On this small island are three shelters that don't see as much use as those at Washington Creek.

From Windigo, you can catch a boat back to Grand Portage or to Rock Harbor Lodge. There is also regular floatplane service to Houghton (see Chapter 4).

7 THE LONG TRAILS

*Minong Ridge • Feldtmann Ridge and Island Mine •
Rock Harbor and Lake Richie*

The Greenstone Ridge Trail is the most popular footpath on the Island but hardly the only one. Within the park are several other long trails that can be combined for a week or even two-week tramp in the woods.

Experienced backpackers who enjoy a little challenge in their hiking would do well to skip the Greenstone and undertake the Minong Ridge Trail. The 26.1 or 27.4-mile trail (depending on whether you include the 1.3-mile Washington Creek Trail at the west end) was originally built in 1966 to give fire fighters access to the north section of the Island. When the trail was opened to visitors, park officials decided to keep it in its rugged and undeveloped state as an alternative to the easy hiking on the Greenstone.

The Minong is definitely an alternative. It stretches along the north shore ridge from McCargoe Cove to Windigo and offers few of the niceties—planking, bridges, trail signs—that most other trails in the park do. When hiking the Minong you inevitably get your boots soaked a few times and occasionally retrace your steps after losing the path. Moose are heavily active in the area, and often their paths will be mistaken for the trail.

But what makes the Minong so demanding is the constant up-and-down hiking over the bare-rock ridge. This quickly wears out the knees and the bottom of your feet and causes aching arches at night. Hikers planning to undertake the trail should arrive in good walking shape, plan on taking an hour to cover a mile, and expect to spend the nights massaging their feet.

The payoff is frequent sightings of wildlife—moose, especially—great views of the north shore and Canada from on top of the ridge, and only a trickle of people. Three of the park's nicest shoreline campgrounds can be used. You could easily spend four days just walking along the Minong Ridge Trail and include stays at McCargoe Cove, Todd Harbor, and Little Todd Harbor campgrounds.

If the desire to seek out solitude excites you but the ruggedness of the Minong Ridge doesn't, tramp the Feldtmann Ridge and Island Mine trails. These trails are well planked, marked, and relatively moderate in difficulty but don't have the use that the Greenstone does. They can be combined with a portion of the Greenstone Ridge and a side trip to Huginnin Cove for a satisfying five-day hike that begins and ends in Windigo.

Highlights of the trip would include the planked trail through the bogs east of Feldtmann Lake, a sunset stroll along beautiful Rainbow Cove, and Siskiwit Bay campground—a pleasant spot to spend a night. Those eager to see signs of wolves or to get the remote opportunity of hearing them howl at night would do well hiking this route.

The third long trail on Isle Royale is the Rock Harbor Trail, a mild-to-

Lake Richie loon nest.

moderate hike that runs from Rock Harbor Lodge along the shoreline to Moskey Basin, 11.2 miles away. Much of the trail is just off the shoreline and can be a very scenic walk. The trail can be combined with the 1.9-mile Lake Richie Trail and portions of the Indian Portage and Greenstone Ridge trails for a circular five-day hike from Rock Harbor Lodge through the northern inland lakes and back.

Rock Harbor Trail can be a busy path, however, especially in midsummer when *Ranger III* pulls in and a stampede of hikers rushes to secure a shelter at Three-Mile or Daisy Farm campgrounds. And if the trail is crowded, the campgrounds will be crowded as well.

MINONG RIDGE TRAIL

Distance: 26.1 or 27.4 miles
Hiking time: 4–5 days
High point: 1047 feet
Rating: difficult

The Minong Ridge is best hiked from east to west, leaving the long portion from Lake Desor to Windigo for the end. Plan on at least 4 hiking days to go from McCargoe Cove to Windigo and no less than 7 to tramp from Rock Harbor Lodge to Windigo.

McCargoe Cove to Todd Harbor

Distance: 6.6 miles

No matter how you arrive at McCargoe Cove, by foot, paddle, or ferryboat, plan on spending a night at the beautiful campground. The site has a half-dozen shelters, individual and group campsites, toilets, and tables. There is also a dock where a pleasant evening can be spent watching beaver, waterfowl, or moose feeding across the cove.

A trail begins from the center of the campground and climbs gently for about 0.5 miles, where it arrives at the junction with the side trail to Minong Mine.

The side trail runs parallel with the Minong Ridge for a short distance until it reaches the site of the Minong Mine, Isle Royal's largest copper mine, operated 1874 to 1883. The area is marked by large piles of rock tailings, rails, and ore cars from the small railroad that hauled rock from several shafts to the cove. Along the way you can spot many small pit mines where prehistoric Indians pounded out pure copper.

The Minong Ridge Trail departs the junction to Minong Mine and ascends steeply for 0.5 miles. At one point you will pass a second junction to the Minong Mine right before the main trail reaches the top of the ridge. Starting here, hikers must be careful to keep an eye out for rock cairns. It is very easy to wander off in the wrong direction and frustrating when you have to backtrack to locate the last marker you passed.

Hikers will also begin the rugged up-and-down trek along the Minong Ridge. For the next mile the trail will follow the ridgetop, and your feet will feel every loose rock you stumble over.

Unexpectedly, Otter Lake appears to the north as a deep blue gem in a green setting. Moose often feed along the shore. The trail drops off the ridge and into a bog and then returns to the crest for another view of the lake. From here it continues along the rocky crest of the Minong Ridge.

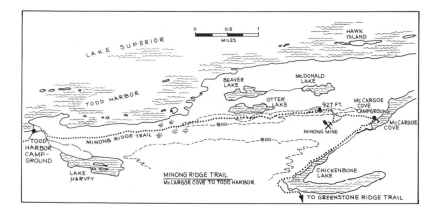

It would be impossible to describe all the dipping and climbing the trail does after leaving Otter Lake, but eventually it passes through another small bog and then climbs sharply. At the ridge top you can see the outlines of Todd Harbor for the first time.

The trail descends again and enters dense forest where it will stay for most of the remaining 2.0 miles to Todd Harbor. Along the way it continues to drop and climb as it passes through bogs, but the hike is considerably easier than the beginning of the hike on the rocky ridge top. Pause and search each bog carefully, for moose often feed there.

Every time the trail climbs over a knoll, quick views of Todd Harbor are possible. Finally, 0.5 miles from the Todd Harbor Campground, the trail takes a northerly swing, crosses a stream, and works its way down to the shore of the harbor.

Todd Harbor is a favorite among backpackers, because the protected water is usually calm and peaceful and the view across the water is stunning during sunsets. The campground has group and individual campsites, pit toilets, and a dock. If a northerly wind is blowing, Todd Harbor will be bug free. Otherwise the campground is known for its outrageous swarms of black flies.

Todd Harbor to Little Todd Harbor

Distance: 6.7 miles

The trail departs Todd Harbor, and in a surprisingly level walk covers the first 1.4 miles in birch forest. It dips only twice to cross streams and then returns to its pleasant stroll—unlike the grunt from McCargoe Cove. After 1.4 miles it reaches the junction of the side trail to Hatchet Lake and the Greenstone Ridge.

The Hatchet Lake Trail swings south to first pass the lakeshore campground (2.3 miles) and eventually reach the Greenstone Ridge Trail (2.6 miles). From the junction of the Hatchet Lake and Minong Ridge trails it is another 5.3 miles to Little Todd Harbor.

The Minong Ridge Trail departs west from the junction of the trail to Hatchet Lake and rises gently back to the ridgetop where it levels out for 0.5 miles. It then descends twice to cross small streams before returning to the ridge. The second stream runs into a scenic little pond where moose like to feed.

After the second stream, the trail climbs sharply to the top of the ridge. Just before reaching the crest, it passes an unmarked, unmaintained side trail that drops 0.5 miles to Pickett Bay, at the west end of Todd Harbor. At the crest you should have your first real scenic views of the day. Through the birch and aspen you can see the Island's north shore, Lake Superior, and Canada.

For the next 1.0 miles the trail closely follows the crest of the Minong Ridge and constantly dips and climbs with it. To the north is a string of swamps and small ponds to view.

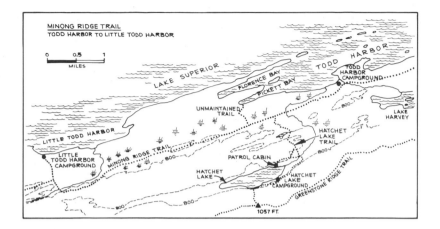

After departing from the open ridge the trail wanders through groves of birch, aspen, and spruce for the next 2.0 miles. The walk continues to tap your energy as it rises and falls with the contours of the land. The patches of forest are broken up by an occasional bog and muddy sections with no planking. There are also some clearings where it might be difficult to see the trail in the heavy underbrush.

Eventually, the trail arrives at a large swamp to the south. Across the bog you should be able to clearly see the Greenstone Ridge. At this point the trail swings to the north, crosses a large stream, and descends sharply off a ridge. The trail swings more easterly, crosses a stream and bog, and climbs another ridge, arriving at the junction with the side trail to Little Todd Harbor.

The side trail to the Little Todd Harbor Campground is a gradual 0.5-mile descent to the shoreline with two steep drops and plankless bogs to cross. The campground is a delight after a tiring day on the Minong Ridge. The individual campsites are near the shoreline, where you can fall asleep to the lapping water of Lake Superior. There is a pit toilet but no group camping.

Little Todd Harbor to North Lake Desor Campground

Distance: 5.7 miles

The section between Little Todd Harbor and the junction of the trail to Lake Desor follows bare ridge most of the way and is the hardest part of the trail. Even a fast hiker in good walking shape will need 4 to 6 hours to cover this stretch.

The trail departs from the junction of the trail to Little Todd Harbor and immediately climbs out of the birch and aspen forest to the rocky crest of the ridge. At the top you should have gained enough elevation for a clear,

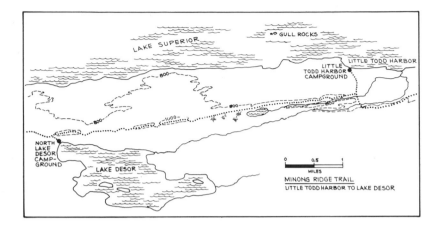

unobstructed view of the Greenstone Ridge to the south, Lake Superior to the north, or more of the ridge straight ahead.

For the next 1.5 miles from the Little Todd Harbor junction the trail follows the open ridge, dipping into forest only twice. Again, a word of caution for hikers: Keep your eye out for the trail markers—rock cairns, orange arrows, or orange tags imbedded in the sides of trees.

After passing a small unnamed lake to the south, the trail drops into forest and continues to climb and dip with the terrain. It returns to another 0.5 miles of open ridge, drops back into forest terrain again, and then steeply climbs to the open ridge where good views of the Greenstone Ridge and Lake Superior are possible.

The trail follows the open ridge for 0.25 miles, drops into forest again, and returns to the rocky crest. Here, for the first time, Lake Desor in all its splendor is visible. This is an encouraging sign for most weary hikers, for now they know they are less than 2.0 miles from the campground.

The trail dips into forest again and climbs back to open ridge before arriving at the junction with the path to North Lake Desor Campground. The side trail drops through the woods to the shoreline 0.5 miles away. The campground has a pit toilet and individual campsites but not too much level ground. There always seems to be a moose—if not several—that run through the campground at dusk or early in the morning.

North Lake Desor Campground to Washington Creek Trail

Distance: 11.4 miles

This section is not as hard as the previous hikes along the Minong Ridge, but usually seems like it because hikers are so eager to reach Windigo. Take your time, and keep your eye on the trail to pick up the occasional rock cairns. This stretch can get confusing when it crosses a couple of beaver ponds.

The trail departs from the junction of the trail to North Lake Desor Campground and immediately climbs to the crest of the ridge, following it for 0.75 miles. It dips only twice into forest during this stretch. After the trail drops into forest a third time, it moves through a large clearing made up mostly of bogs and meadows.

The trail follows the all-too-common pattern of climbing to the ridge, dropping into the forest, returning to the ridge, dropping to a bog, returning to the ridge, and so on. This goes on for a spell, but several of the wettest swamps are planked.

Eventually the trail arrives at a small pond and crosses it on a bridge that looks like a beaver dam. The trail swings to the right and immediately climbs up and over a small ridge before dropping to a second pond. This one is studded with standing dead trees, the result of beavers damming the stream and flooding the area. Although it may not seem like it, this pond is also crossed on a log-and-mud dam that cuts north across the pond.

The trail climbs the ridge on the other side of the pond and then begins a gradual descent through forest terrain to Washington Creek Basin. There are a few final dips and drops in the trail before it winds gently through a yellow-birch forest and then descends sharply to Washington Creek and the surrounding bog.

The creek is crossed by a wooden bridge; on the other side, hikers are greeted by a *Minong Trail* sign. The Minong Trail officially ends here, and you are now on the Washington Creek Trail. Another 100 yards west is the Wendigo Mine exploration site, where the last attempt to find profitable copper on the Island was made.

The trail heads west along a level path that passes several bogs, all planked. As the trail nears Washington Creek Campground it passes three junctions. The first is 0.9 miles past the Wendigo Mine exploration site and

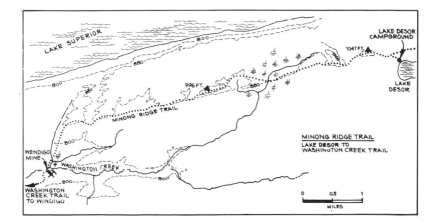

1.3 miles outside of Windigo. This side trail is the eastern loop to Huginnin Cove, 3.8 miles on the north shore.

The next junction is the western loop to Huginnin Cove (3.4 miles), another 0.3 miles down Washington Creek Trail and 1.0 miles east of Windigo.

The final junction, 0.3 miles outside Washington Creek Campground and 0.7 miles east of Windigo, is the western end of the Greenstone Ridge Trail.

FELDTMANN RIDGE AND ISLAND MINE TRAILS

Distance: 22.2 miles
Hiking time: 3 days
High point: 1200 feet
Rating: moderate

The Feldtmann Ridge–Island Mine circuit is a pleasant walk that takes you into the southwest part of the park—perhaps the most desolate corner of Isle Royale. Researchers believe that many of the wolves reside in this area during the summer.

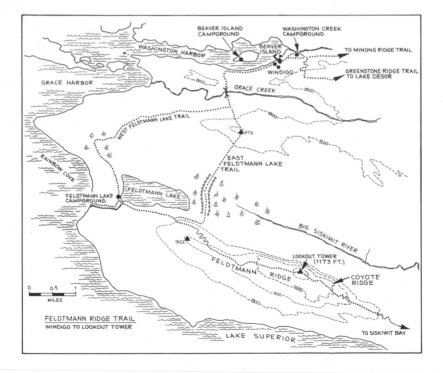

Pond and bog swamp, off Huginnin Cove Loop.

The only steep climbs in the hike are over the Feldtmann and Greenstone ridges; the rest of the trek tends to be relatively level. Many backpackers like to hike to Feldtmann Lake Campground first, making the final day a downhill walk along the Greenstone Ridge to Windigo. One difficult part of the trail is the 10.3-mile hike from Feldtmann Lake Campground to Siskiwit Bay. The trek, which involves crossing the Feldtmann Ridge, can be long and tiring.

The first part of the trail, from Windigo to the junction of the trail to Feldtmann Campground (5.6 miles), is also known as the East Feldtmann Lake Trail.

Windigo to Feldtmann Lake Campground

Distance: 7.1 miles

Start in front of the Windigo visitor center and follow the road west to the trail head. The first 1.0 miles of the trail are a beautiful stretch that hugs the Washington Harbor shoreline and provides constant views of the harbor, Beaver Island, and various waterfowl that hang around the shore.

After passing Beaver Island and a small boat marker on the harbor, the trail swings sharply south and climbs what remains of the Greenstone Ridge. It drops off the low ridge into a planked bog and crosses the bridge over Grace Creek, 1.5 miles from Windigo. For those with the time and desire, it is possible to hike down the creek toward its mouth at Grace Harbor. The creek is known for its excellent brook-trout fishing and frequent visits by feeding moose.

When walking through the bogs, you will see a variety of prints. At times there are more moose prints in the mud than human footprints. The trail leaves the bog and climbs a small ridge, where it arrives at the junction with the West Feldtmann Lake Trail, 2.0 miles out of Windigo. The West Feldtmann Lake Trail swings around the backside of the lake to the campground, 6.7 miles away. From this point, Windigo is 2.3 miles to the north and Feldtmann Ridge is 3.3 miles to the south.

From the junction the trail continues to climb until it reaches a high point of 973 feet. It then drops sharply into a flat and very pleasant open area and remains in it for 1.5 miles. Moose will often be seen wandering through, especially near the east end of Feldtmann Lake. For those with sharp eyes, an occasional wolf track might also be found along the trail.

At the head of Feldtmann Lake the trail crosses an alder swamp along a planked boardwalk 1200 feet long, the longest in the park. This area is an interesting change from the forest-covered trails elsewhere in the park. To the east is Siskiwit Swamp, the largest morass on the Island, covering more than 10 square miles.

While moving through the swamp, Feldtmann Ridge comes into view to the south.The high bluffs take on a reddish color in places, caused by the conglomerate rock they are composed of, and are topped by what looks like a single line of white pines. The trail heads straight for the ridge and then turns west when it reaches its base. The trail follows the base for 0.5 miles until reaching the junction with the trail to Feldtmann Lake Campground.

The side trail to the campground runs along the south shore of the lake for 1.5 miles. After 0.75 miles, the trail swings close enough to the lake for eager fishermen to bushwhack to the shoreline. Feldtmann is one of the finest northern pike lakes in the park.

The campground is on the southwest corner of the lake and has individual and group campsites and pit toilets. The campground is nice and is next to the 1.0-mile trail to Rainbow Cove (see Chapter 14).

Feldtmann Lake Campground to Siskiwit Bay

Distance: 10.3 miles

This is a long hike, one that backpackers should begin early in the day and not try to rush through. Begin by backtracking the 1.5 miles from the campground to the junction at the base of the Feldtmann Ridge. At this point the Feldtmann Ridge Lookout Tower is 3.3 miles away, and Siskiwit Bay is 8.8 miles.

From here the Feldtmann Ridge Trail climbs sharply for several hundred yards until it arrives at the top of the ridge. The views can be spectacular once you reach the crest. Below is Feldtmann Lake, while far off to the west is Grace Harbor and Rock of Ages Lighthouse. To the east you can see Siskiwit Bay and the Greenstone Ridge. Be careful not to venture too close to the edge of the steep ridge: Much of the rock is undercut at the dropoff.

The trail continues along the ridge, dipping and climbing as it makes a gradual ascent to Mount Feldtmann and the lookout tower. It winds through stands of birch and mountain ash and openings caused by the forest fire of 1936. About 1.0 miles from the junction it nears a bog where

Feldtmann Ridge Lookout Tower. (Photo by Steve and Carol Maass)

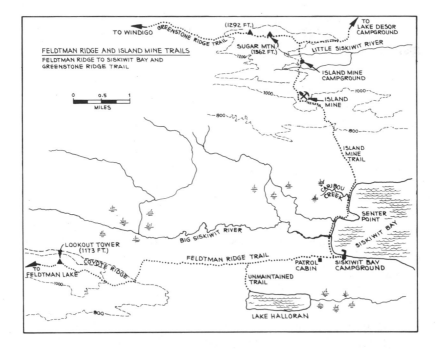

there is a small beaver dam and pond to the south.

The trail continues to climb for another 2.0 miles, winds through one last stand of birch, and then arrives at the lookout tower 8.9 miles from Windigo. The view from the tower is excellent. You can see almost the entire western half of the Island, including Big Siskiwit Swamp, Sugar Mountain, and the Greenstone Ridge; to the northeast, Siskiwit Bay and Lake Halloran are visible.

After departing from the lookout tower, the trail descends for a short spell and quickly climbs again, first passing an old unmarked trail to a spring and then arriving near the top of Coyote Ridge. Here you will see remains of an old log fire tower.

The trail then drops rapidly off the ridge, swings to a northerly direction, and enters a lowland. It makes another swing to the northeast and becomes part of an old logging road built in the 1930s. In this area, the trail follows a terrace where it is easy to envision the old beach line of Lake Superior. At one time in the formation of Isle Royale, Big Siskiwit River Valley was under water—a part of Lake Superior. Feldtmann Ridge and much of the land to the south was an island.

A little more than 1.5 miles after the trail swings to the northeast, it passes the unmaintained side trail to Lake Halloran. The trail—1.7 miles west of Siskiwit Bay Campground—is no longer marked. But those with the time or who want to take a day hike out of Siskiwit Bay Campground can hunt for the trail and follow it 0.5 miles to the rectangular lake. Halloran is known for it fine northern-pike fishing and the orchids that grow along the shoreline.

The last leg of the trail is enjoyable because it is level and winds through open meadows. Just before reaching Siskiwit Bay, you pass through a grassy area that was the site of a Civilian Conservation Corps (CCC) camp in the 1930s. A little farther on, before entering the campground, you arrive at the junction with the Island Mine Trail.

The Siskiwit Bay Campground is a pleasant spot to spend a night or even an extra day. The trail crews have dubbed the spot "Riviera of Isle Royale." It features warmer air and water temperatures than much of the park and has long stretches of red sandstone beach. The campground has two shelters, group and individual campsites, tables, pit toilets, grills, and a large dock.

Siskiwit Bay to Greenstone Ridge

Distance: 4.8 miles

The 5.0-mile Island Mine Trail is a historical walk through much of the park's past. You could probably hike from Siskiwit Bay to the Greenstone Ridge in 3 hours or spend an entire day exploring the artifacts in the brush alongside the trail.

From the junction with the path to Feldtmann Ridge, the trail departs north toward the Greenstone Ridge. At this point the Greenstone Ridge Trail lies 4.7 miles to the north and Windigo 14.4 miles west, along the Feldtmann Ridge Trail.

The first 1.5 miles of the Island Mine Trail are a beautiful walk circling the west end of Siskiwit Bay. Most of the time the trail is just inside the brush off the beach. If hiking in the early morning, you might want to walk along the beach to avoid getting soaked by wet underbrush.

The trail crosses bridges over two forks of the Big Siskiwit River and then arrives at Senter Point. The trail crosses the neck of the point, which was used by the Island Mine Company in the 1870s to store their explosives. Just before reaching the beach on the north side of the point, you can hike a short way toward the end of the point and see the remains of the company's stone powder house.

North of Senter Point the trail follows the beach to its northern end where it swings northwest and moves inland. At this spot the mining company built a town that housed the workers and serviced the mines 2.0 miles north. The company constructed a wagon road from the camp to the shafts where 213,245 pounds of refined copper were mined from 1874 to 1878.

It is the bed of the wagon road that the trail follows for the next 2.0 miles—and makes for easy hiking. The first 1.0 miles inland are a level walk through wet lowlands, mostly of spruce and fir. After crossing a bridge over a small creek, the trail begins to climb.

Those interested in the trees and forests of the Island will marvel at this spot, because the creek marks a transition in the make-up of the woods. The trail leaves the cool, moist valley of spruce, fir, and paper birch and climbs a south-facing slope exposed to long hours of sunlight. In this dry, warm terrain sugar maples and northern red oaks take over as the predominant trees.

The trail climbs for 0.75 miles where it passes an old well, climbs for another 0.75 miles, and arrives at the Island Mine. What remains are large piles of rock tailings, evidence that this was the second largest mining operation on the Island. If you poke around the area, be careful of the old shafts and pits.

The wagon road ended here, and the trail now departs from the mining site as a much more narrow and rugged path. It descends into a depression of spruce–fir forest and quickly climbs another ridge. From the low ridge the trail drops again, crosses a stream, and begins its final climb through luxuriant sugar-maple–yellow-birch forest to Island Mine Campground.

Some backpackers spend the evening at Island Mine Campground (see Chapter 7), and others prefer to hike the 6.0 miles downhill along the Greenstone Ridge to Windigo. To reach the Greenstone, hike through the campground. The trail descends into a bog and then makes a sharp climb to the top of the ridge, where it ends at the junction with the Greenstone Ridge Trail, 0.5 miles from the campground. From here the Windigo Ranger Station is 6.5 miles to the west, and Lake Desor Campground is 5.2 miles to the east on the Greenstone Ridge Trail.

ROCK HARBOR AND LAKE RICHIE TRAILS

Distance: 13.1 miles
Hiking time: 2–3 days
High point: 726 feet
Rating: easy to moderate

The Rock Harbor Trail is undoubtedly the most rerouted trail in the park. Originally, it ran from Rock Harbor Lodge along the shoreline to Moskey Basin. But heavy traffic caused rapid erosion, and park officials moved it inland 0.5 miles from Three-Mile Campground to the end. At this writing it's back along the shore to Daisy Farm Campground, where it moves inland the rest of the way.

The first part is a mild walk along the bluffs of the shoreline, with constant views of the water. If just stepping off *Ranger III* or *Isle Royale Queen*, you can hike to Three-Mile Campground in 1½–2 hours. Daisy Farm Campground is another 2½–3 hours away.

The last part to Moskey Basin is more difficult and tiring. Though the trail doesn't climb any great ridge, it does cover a rocky terrain in a constant up-and-down fashion.

Restored Pete Edisen Fish Camp across from Daisy Farm Campground.

Rock Harbor Lodge to Three-Mile Campground

Distance: 2.9 miles

At Rock Harbor Lodge, follow the path through the campground to the beginning of the trail. It is a well-worn footpath that departs from the campground and winds through spruce forest for a short spell before breaking out on a bluff above the water.

The trail remains close to the shore, crossing many rock bluffs with minimal climbing and dipping back into the woods in between. Watch for rock cairns on the rocky bluffs, and be careful when it is raining. The bluffs can get extremely slippery. About 0.75 miles from Rock Harbor Lodge, the trail dips to waterline and then right back above it again.

A sign to Suzy's Cave appears 1.8 miles from the beginning of the trail. The inland sea arch is about 80 yards to the north and provides an excellent viewing point of the Rock Harbor waterway. In another 1.1 miles the trail arrives at Three-Mile Campground.

The campground is pleasant, situated right off the shoreline, and is a quiet alternative to the one at Rock Harbor Lodge. There are eight shelters, group and individual camping, pit toilets, and a dock.

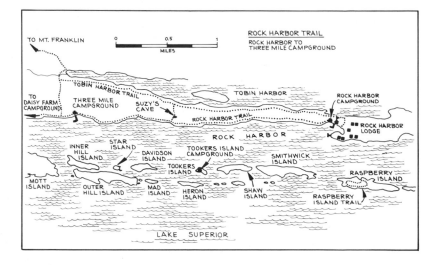

Three-Mile Campground to Daisy Farm Campground

Distance: 4.4 miles

Just west of Three-Mile Campground the trail arrives at the junction of the side trail to Mount Franklin. The scenic mountain peak lies 2.3 miles to the north on the side trail; Daisy Farm Campground is 4.4 miles west along Rock Harbor Trail.

The trail departs from the junction and continues its course along the side of Rock Harbor. At one point it reaches a rock bluff, and across the channel you can see the cove on Mott Island where the NPS barges are docked. After another 1.0 miles or so, you stand opposite the NPS head-quarters on Mott Island.

Shortly after that, the trail passes the remains of the Siskiwit Mine, 1.8 miles from Three-Mile Campground. There are several fenced-off shafts in the area and the stone foundations of former buildings the miners built. Caution should be used when investigating the shafts.

The rest of the walk to Daisy Farm Campground is a very pleasant and level 2.0 miles. At times the trail crosses clearings where you should be able first to see Caribou Island Campground and then Rock Harbor Lighthouse and Edisen Fishery. About 0.25 miles from Daisy Farm you will spot the long dock jutting out in the channel.

Daisy Farm is a shoreline campground that falls in the same category as the ones at Rock Harbor Lodge and Windigo. It's a very popular spot to spend a night or even a couple of days and consequently has a lot of traffic through it. Originally, it was the site of a town called Ransom and later was used as a vegetable farm (thus the name "Daisy Farm") for Rock Harbor Lodge. In the 1930s, the CCC also had a camp here.

Red squirrel.

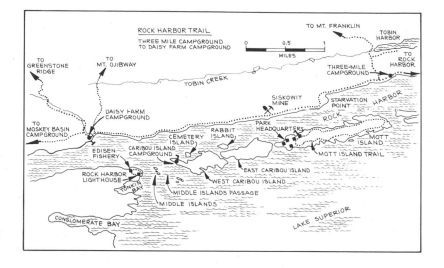

The campground has 15 shelters (often taken by early afternoon) and group and individual campsites. Backpackers will also find pit toilets, piped-in water, tables, and even a covered picnic area. There is a ranger stationed there who gives evening talks most of the summer.

Daisy Farm Campground to Moskey Basin

Distance: 3.9 miles

The Rock Harbor Trail follows the Daisy Farm Trail as it departs from the campground and heads northwest for the Greenstone Ridge. After 0.2 miles you arrive at the junction where the two trails split.

The Rock Harbor Trail heads west, and in 0.25 miles from the junction passes an unmarked path that wanders a few yards up a rock outcrop. You should take a moment to walk to the edge, for it provides the only glimpse of Moskey Basin you'll have on the entire trek.

From here the trail begins its up-and-down course over one rocky crest after another for almost the entire way to Moskey Basin Campground. A few times it dips down into wooded terrain, only to break out and ascend another bare rocky crest. Keep sharp eyes out for rock cairns or rocks painted orange, because it is easy to lose the trail.

Eventually, 1.0 miles from Moskey Basin, the trail departs from the rocky ridges and descends into forest, where it remains except for climbing over one last small crest. The trail approaches a steep ridge a short way from the campground, turns west, and runs parallel to the ridge for 100 yards before dipping down to the junction with Lake Richie Trail.

At this junction, Lake Richie lies 2.0 miles to the west, Daisy Farm is 3.7 miles to the east, and Moskey Basin Campground is 0.2 miles across an unnamed stream to the south. Moskey Basin is a beautiful campground situated right off the well-protected waters at the end of Rock Harbor. There are six shelters, group and individual campsites, pit toilets, a large dock, and some incredible sunrises. The campground is truly the gem of Rock Harbor.

From Moskey Basin you could hike the Lake Richie Trail to the Indian Portage Trail, which would take you to the Greenstone Ridge. Once on the Greenstone you could circle back to Rock Harbor Lodge or head west to reach Windigo in 3 or 4 days. You would need another 2 or 3 days to reach Rock Harbor Lodge and 4 days to hike to Windigo.

Lake Richie Trail

Distance: 1.9 miles

From the junction with the Rock Harbor Trail north of the unnamed stream, the path to Lake Richie departs west and runs parallel to the stream for a short distance. It passes a bog, dips and climbs through the spruce–fir forest, and eventually climbs its first ridge.

The ridge is low and the walk easy compared to the stretch from Daisy Farm to Moskey Basin. The trail follows the contour of the ridge for a spell, descends, and then climbs a second ridge. It stays on the crest of this ridge even longer than the first time, reaches a high point of 726 feet, and then makes a sharp descent. Here the Lake Richie Trail officially ends at the junction with the Indian Portage Trail, which heads south for 4.2 miles to Chippewa Harbor Campground.

From the junction you wander west on the Indian Portage Trail for another 0.1 miles to the shoreline of Lake Richie. The Lake Richie Campground is another 0.1 miles farther on.

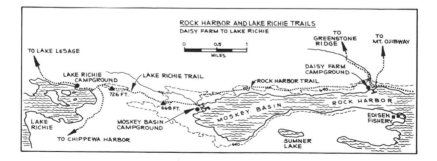

8 THE SHORT TRAILS, WEST

Huginnin Cove Loop • *West Feldtmann Lake* •
Windigo Nature Walk • *Washington Creek*

Windigo is a nice place, but if you have a spare day, don't spend it hanging around the camp store. There are several short trails in the area that make pleasant day hikes, and two can be turned into overnight excursions to escape the bustling Washington Creek Campground.

The most popular side trail is Huginnin Cove Loop, a 9.5-mile round trip out of Windigo. This mild trail loops through the northwest corner of the park and passes through the secluded and scenic Huginnin Cove, a good place to watch a sunset.

The West Feldtmann Lake Trail is also near Windigo. It begins 2.3 miles out on the Feldtmann Ridge Trail and winds 6.0 miles to the back (west) side of the lake. When combined with a portion of the Feldtmann Ridge route (or East Feldtmann Lake Trail), this pair of trails make for an ideal 2-day hike, one that will almost guarantee a northern-pike dinner at night.

And if you are looking for a way to use up the last few hours before the ferryboat or plane arrives, there is the short Windigo Nature Walk or the 2.0-mile stroll out to the Wendigo Mine exploration site along the Washington Creek Trail.

HUGINNIN COVE LOOP TRAIL

Distance: 9.5-mile round trip from Windigo
Hiking time: 4–6 hours
High point: 847 feet
Rating: easy

The loop to Huginnin Cove is an excellent overnight trip that requires 2–4 hours of hiking each way. Although there are some ridges to climb, none is steep and the trail overall is easy—unless it rains. Then it becomes more difficult because several bogs swell in size, and the planking, old and deteriorating in spots, becomes slippery and hard to cross.

Moose frequent the swamps and ponds along the trail, and there are brook trout in Huginnin Creek near the campground. But have your insect repellent handy. The cove has its share of gnats and deer flies.

From Windigo take the Washington Creek Trail to the first junction of the trail to Huginnin Cove—an easy 1-mile walk. From this point the cove lies 3.4 miles to the north. The eastern loop begins another 0.3 miles down Washington Creek Trail.

From the junction the West Huginnin Cove Trail descends for 0.25 miles until it crosses a bridge over Washington Creek. Next to the bridge is a small gauging station that houses instruments used to measure the flow of the creek. From here the trail climbs through open hillside before dropping again to cross a second stream.

The trail now begins to swing to the west as it ascends another open hillside. After battling with the thick underbrush, you dip into forest and arrive at a nice view of Washington Harbor through the trees. There will be more glimpses of the harbor as the trail continues west, following the hilly terrain and eventually making a steep climb to the ridgetop.

The trail dips and climbs with the ridge for about 0.5 miles before curving to the north and revealing a large ravine. This is a fault line, and the trail follows it right to the north shore. You stay on the ridge on the east side before dropping to cross a planked bog.

After climbing again, the trail descends a second time and passes a small beaver pond. It stays on the floor of this trough, travels through open areas for a while, and then crosses to the ridge on the west side. The trail climbs into the ridge and then begins to descend to the cove. At the end the trail follows the west bank of the Huginnin Creek and turns into a well-padded path as it enters the campground.

The campground is right off the shore of this beautiful and secluded cove. There is no group camping but there are a handful of individual sites,

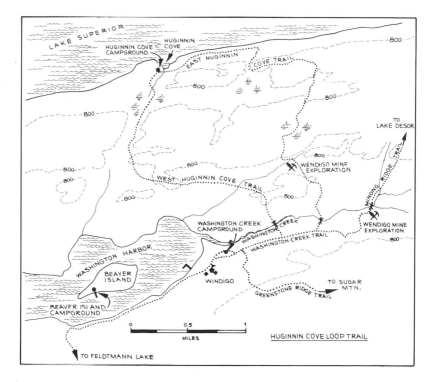

a pit toilet, and a small beach to wander along. It is also possible to scramble over the rocks and climb to the cove west of Huginnin, where there are large flat rocks that are ideal sites for sunbathing.

Huginnin Cove to Washington Creek

Distance: 3.8 miles

Near the campground, next to Huginnin Creek, is the junction of the two trails to the cove. From here Washington Creek Trail lies 3.4 miles away on the western loop or 3.8 miles on the eastern portion.

The East Huginnin Cove Loop leaves the junction, crosses the creek, and then hugs the north shore for almost 1.0 miles. This is by far the most interesting section of the hike. There are great views of Lake Superior and the steep cliffs that make up much of the north shore.

Eventually, the trail turns south, climbs steeply to a ridge top, and swings back east as it follows the ridge. The trail then descends into a marsh that is ideal for spotting moose. You cross this marsh on some poor planking, gently rise into forested terrain, and pass an old log cabin left over from the mining days.

The trail breaks out into a second and larger marsh. It skirts around the pond and climbs into forest before descending steadily to the remains of the Wendigo mine exploration, 0.25 miles from the second swamp. There is evidence of mining everywhere in this area, and a quick search can reveal steel rails, old log cabins, and several exploration pits camouflaged by thick vegetation.

From the old mine exploration site, the trail winds around another swamp, makes a short climb to a ridge top, and then begins its long drop to Washington Creek. Before reaching a bridge over the creek, the trail winds through the swamp on the north side. This is a popular moose area, and there will be many moose paths cutting across the trail.

From the creek it is a short uphill climb to the second junction with Washington Creek Trail. From here, Windigo lies 1.3 miles to the west, and the Wendigo Mine exploration site and the start of the Minong Ridge Trail are 0.7 miles to the east.

WEST FELDTMANN LAKE TRAIL

Distance: 6.7 miles
High point: 720 feet
Hiking time: 3–5 hours
Rating: moderate

The West Feldtmann Lake Trail begins at a junction with the Feldtmann Ridge Trail (or East Feldtmann Lake Trail) 2.3 miles out of Windigo and makes a 6.7-mile swing to the southwest corner of the rectangular lake.

Wendigo Mine buildings, about 1892. (Fisher Collection photo, Michigan Technological University Archives)

When combined with the first portion of the Feldtmann Ridge Trail (see map on page 68), it makes for a 2-day hike to the Feldtmann Lake Campground and is highlighted by the fine northern-pike fishing in the semi-isolated lake.

But if you are passing through on your way to Siskiwit Bay, take the Feldtmann Ridge Trail. West Feldtmann Lake Trail is a long walk that is rather uninspiring in its scenery. The only time a hiker should choose it is when there has been a heavy rainfall and the ridge trail is in poor condition. The west trail is relatively level and dry because it follows old beach lines much of the way.

The junction to the West Feldtmann Lake Trail is on a ridge 0.5 miles past the bridge over Grace Creek. From here the Feldtmann Lake Campground is 6.7 miles along the west trail or 4.8 miles on the ridge route.

The West Feldtmann Lake Trail heads west for more than 3.0 miles, staying in forest terrain but occasionally crossing a planked bog. The trail then makes a wide swing to the south, and old beach lines—formed when glaciers kept Lake Superior at a higher level—become very distinct. One and one-half miles from the campground, the beach lines give you the impression of walking below Feldtmann Lake.

The trail runs near the west shore of the lake in the final 1.0 miles before arriving at the junction with two other trails in the middle of the campground. Rainbow Cove is 0.8 miles to the west (see Chapter 14), and the other trail heads east around the south side of the lake to Feldtmann Ridge Trail, 1.5 miles away.

Feldtmann Lake Campground is near the shore of the lake and offers group camping, individual campsites, and pit toilets. The campground is within easy walking distance of Rainbow Cove—a beautiful body of water, especially during dusk. Shore fishermen should take the trail to Feldtmann Ridge for a short distance, and then cut to the lake. There are several productive weed beds along the south shore.

WINDIGO NATURE WALK

Distance: 1.2 miles
Hiking time: 30 minutes
Rating: easy

This trail (and the Washington Creek Trail) is an easy trail near Windigo and good for loosening up your legs before the boat ride home. The nature walk is a self-guiding stroll that begins near the store. It passes by an old beach shore, a moose study enclosure, birch forest, and moose sign in the form of droppings, prints, and stripped aspen and fir trees.

WASHINGTON CREEK TRAIL

Distance: 2.0 miles
Hiking time: 1 hour
Rating: easy

Washington Creek Trail begins at the visitor center and heads east for 2.0 miles to the start of the Minong Ridge Trail. After passing Washington Creek Campground to the left and an old beach line to the right, this trail arrives at the junction with the Greenstone Ridge Trail.

The junction to the first Huginnin Cove Trail is reached 1.0 miles from Windigo, and the second trail is passed in another 0.3 miles. From here the trail remains level as it passes through forest terrain and an occasional planked bog.

After one noticeably long planked section over a bog, the trail swings to the northeast and finally arrives at the Wendigo Mine exploration site, little more than a shallow cave in the side of a rock bluff. From here it is another 100 yards to the start of the Minong Trail.

9 THE SHORT TRAILS, CENTRAL

Indian Portage and Lake Mason • Ishpeming •
East Chickenbone • Hatchet Lake

These trails are in the central portion of the park and are usually com-bined with portions of the Greenstone and Minong Ridge routes for a vari-ety of week-long tramps. Because they all basically run north to south, they involve hiking over several ridges. The trails can be tiring at times, but none of them is near the difficulty of the Minong Ridge Trail.

The Indian Portage Trail, from Chippewa Harbor to McCargoe Cove, is the only path on the Island that comes close to going from shore to shore. It is a scenic trail and a fisherman's delight as it winds through the north-ern inland lakes, touching the waters of Richie, LeSage, Livermore, and Chickenbone. The 10.7-mile route is used extensively by paddlers portaging their boats across the park.

The Ishpeming Trail winds 7.3 miles from Malone Bay Campground around the west end of Siskiwit Lake to the Ishpeming Point on the Green-stone Ridge. The trail allows hikers to reach Malone Bay, one of the park's most pleasant campgrounds. Unfortunately, unless you see intra-island transportation, the only way out is to rehike the trail.

The East Chickenbone Trail is a 1.6-mile route along the back (east) side of the lake, from the Greenstone Ridge Trail to the Indian Portage Trail just outside McCargoe Cove. The Hatchet Lake Trail is a 2.6-path that connects the Greenstone Ridge to the Minong Ridge, passing the Hatchet Lake Campground and two side trails to a NPS patrol cabin.

INDIAN PORTAGE
AND LAKE MASON TRAILS

Distance: 10.7 miles
High point: 800 feet
Hiking time: 7–10 hours
Rating: moderate

It is believed that Indians used this route to portage their birch-bark canoes from one harbor to another across the Island. The Civilian Conser-vation Corps built this trail in the 1930s, and today the northern portion from Lake Richie to McCargoe Cove sees much use from fishermen, hikers, and canoeists. Not as many visitors travel along the southern por-tion, because it dead ends at Chippewa Harbor.

The path traverses just about every type of terrain found in the park. Along the way you will pass lakes, swamps, and beaver ponds. You will

Swamps like this are a good place to watch for wildlife.

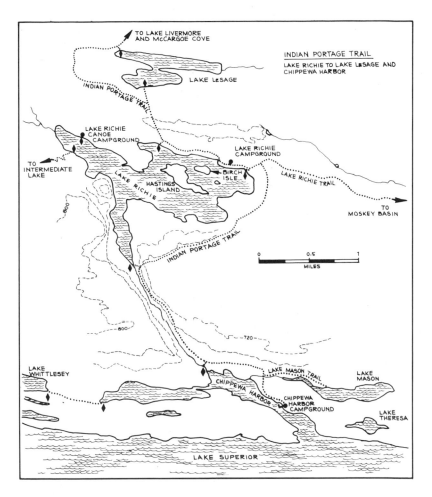

climb ridges and pass through dense forest and sections still scarred by the 1936 fire. Most hikers arrive either on the Greenstone Ridge or the Rock Harbor Trail and head north or south on Indian Portage at this point. To accommodate all hikers, the trail will be described from Lake Richie north to McCargoe Cove and Lake Richie South to Chippewa Harbor.

Lake Richie to McCargoe Cove

Distance: 6.5 miles

The Lake Richie Trail runs from Moskey Basin Campground to a junction with the Indian Portage Trail, 0.2 miles from the east shore of Lake Richie. At this point the Greenstone Ridge Trail lies 3.6 miles to the north and Chippewa Harbor Campground is 4.2 miles to the south.

From this junction the Indian Portage Trail heads west to the shoreline of the lake and follows it closely for a short way. It then arrives at the Lake Richie Campground, situated up in the woods off the lake.

The campground has individual and group campsites and pit toilets. Some individual campsites are on a bluff with a nice view of the lake below. Others are stuck back in the woods, where bugs can be a problem.

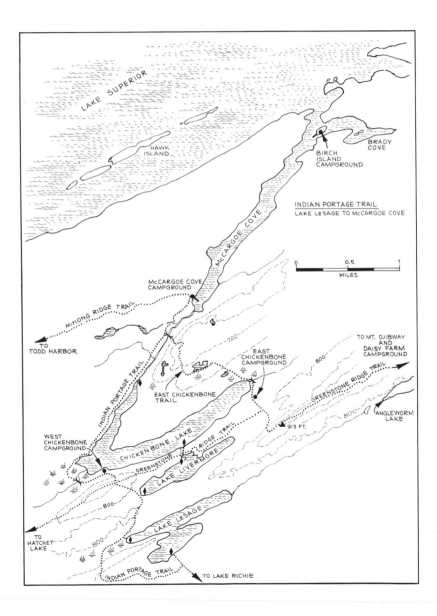

INDIAN PORTAGE TRAIL
LAKE LeSAGE TO McCARGOE COVE

The campground is a favorite among visitors because it offers excellent shore fishing nearby and a good chance to spot moose in the early morning or at dusk.

From the campground the trail winds for almost 1.0 miles on a bluff that forms the north shore of the lake. This is a very pleasant section because the walk is easy and the views of Lake Richie and the small islands that dot it are excellent.

Eventually, the trail swings north, climbs and levels out on a ridge, and then drops down to the swamps bordering Lake LeSage. At this point the trail arrives at a junction with a side trail that wanders ahead over a small hump to the shore of Lake LeSage. Canoeists and kayakers take the side trail and put-in to paddle straight across the lake.

Hikers are not so lucky, and they must follow Indian Portage Trail as it swings to the west. The trail crosses a ridge, drops to a bog, and then crosses another low ridge. Here, it drops through another bog and swings to the second arm of Lake LeSage, where there is another short side trail to the lake for paddlers looking for a put-in or shore fishermen looking for dinner.

The trail departs from Lake LeSage and gently climbs a ridge. After crossing the top of the ridge, the trail drops sharply to the portage marker at the western end of Lake Livermore. From here the trail swings away from the lake and climbs sharply to the top of the Greenstone Ridge.

Here, the choices are many at this major junction. The Hatchet Lake Campground is 7.7 miles to the west, and Daisy Farm Campground is 7.7 to the east on the Greenstone Ridge Trail. North at the end of the Indian Portage Trail is McCargoe Cove, 2.9 miles away.

After departing from the Greenstone Ridge, the trail drops rapidly for 0.25 miles to West Chickenbone Campground on the shores of the lake (see Chapter 6). It winds through the campground along the shoreline and heads into a bog at the west end of the lake. The trail crosses the swamp and stream along a planked walk and then returns to the lake shore.

Here, it follows the northern arm of Chickenbone for a beautiful hike. On a clear day the lake is a mass of blue, highlighted by loons and beavers swimming and painted turtles sunning themselves along the shore. The trail always keeps the lake in sight as it follows the arm to the portage sign at the end.

The trail departs from the lake and follows Chickenbone Creek to Mc-Cargoe Cove, passing a handful of old beaver dams along the way. The arm, creek, and the cove are in a depression that was part of an ancient geologic fault cutting diagonally across the Island. For the most part the trail stays up on the ridge of the fault but does drop to the stream a couple of times for a little up and down hiking in the final mile.

One-half mile from McCargoe Cove the trail passes the junction with the East Chickenbone Trail, which leads back 1.6 miles to East Chickenbone Campground.

Just before arriving at the cove, you'll pass a flat sandy area to the right. This was caused by the stamp mill the miners built 40 yards up the ridge.

The mill crushed ore that was brought from the mines 0.5 miles away on a narrow-gauge railroad and disposed of the stamp sand by allowing it to wash down the hill. The open area was later used by the miners as a stable for their horses. Little remains today that shows the intense activity that characterized the area a century ago.

Lake Richie to Chippewa Harbor

Distance: 4.2 miles

The other half of Indian Portage Trail departs south from the junction with the Lake Richie Trail and immediately swings away from the lake. Here, it remains for about two miles, climbing over the old burned slopes of the 1936 forest fire. Eventually the trail shifts toward the southwest and arrives at a junction with a short side trail. This trail leads back to the portage marker at the end of the southern arm of Lake Richie.

From the lake's arm, the trail follows the drainage creek along the ridge to the beginning of Chippewa Harbor. There is much dipping and climbing in this 1.0-mile section, but twice the trail reaches high on the ridge where the trees thin out; there are possible peeks of the other side of the ravine.

From the second high point the trail begins to drop and passes through

Ishpeming Trail bridge, west end of Siskiwit Lake. (Photo by Steve and Carol Maass)

a narrow gorge, where the rapids from the nearby stream can be heard but not seen unless you wander into the woods. The trail descends even more sharply until it reaches the put-in for canoeists and kayakers portaging their boats from Lake Richie to Chippewa Harbor.

After passing the portage marker, the trail climbs another ridge, reaches the top, and levels out. Here, the trees are still scrubby—another sign of the 1936 forest fire. On your left (or to the northeast) is a long bog with a large pond where you may see moose feeding. From the ridge, the trail swings due south and begins its descent to Chippewa Harbor.

Right before reaching the campground the trail passes the side trail to Lake Mason. The side trail takes about 20 minutes to cover one way and is an easy 0.7-mile walk to the rock bluff that overlooks the entire lake.

Chippewa Harbor Campground is another favorite for hikers because its four shelters are situated high above the water, with a good view of the harbor. The narrow entrance from Lake Superior, surrounded by rugged bluffs and small islands, is especially beautiful. The campground also has individual and group campsites, pit toilets, tables, and a dock.

ISHPEMING TRAIL

Distance: 7.6 miles
High point: 1377 feet
Hiking time: 4–6 hours
Rating: moderate to difficult

The trail winds from Malone Bay Campground to Ishpeming Point on the Greenstone Ridge, climbing over three major ridges along the way. The constant up and down terrain makes the hike more difficult than most trails on the Island.

Ishpeming Point, which to the Chippewa Indians meant "heaven," is the second highest point on the Island (1377 feet). The views are uninspiring, however, because only the west end of Siskiwit Bay is visible through the trees. Lying to the east and west from this point are Lake Desor and Hatchet Lake campgrounds, both approximately 4.0 miles away.

The Ishpeming Trail departs from the lookout tower and immediately begins its long descent from the Greenstone Ridge. At times the trail is steep and wanders over bare rock surfaces, where it is easy to lose the path. After 0.75 miles, the trail finally bottoms out, crosses a bog and small stream that are planked, and begins a steep ascent.

This time the trail peaks at 1123 feet before descending off the ridge into a bog still scarred by the 1936 forest fire. After passing through the bog the trail begins to climb again and reaches 1088 feet on Red Oak Ridge. From the top there are views of Siskiwit Bay; the forest changes from yellow birch to large stands of sugar maple, northern red oak, and white pine.

The trail gradually descends from the ridge by heading east before turn-

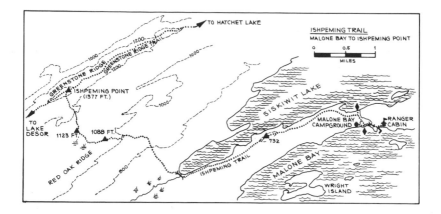

ing south for the western end of Siskiwit Lake. It continues to drop for more than 1.0 miles from Red Oak Ridge before leveling out in birch–aspen forest. After another 0.75 miles, the trail crosses a planked bog and small stream and then quickly arrives at a second stream.

This one connects Mud Lake with Siskiwit Lake and is crossed on an old wooden bridge. From the middle of the bridge you can view the western end of Isle Royale's largest lake. The trail departs from the bridge and immediately swings to the east. It follows the lake shore for another 3.0 miles through a paper-birch forest.

There is an occasional view of the lake through the trees, and about halfway along the shore you climb up and over a small knoll. The trail passes a bog right before arriving at the Malone Bay boat landing on Siskiwit Lake. Near the landing and portage marker is a stream that forms the beautiful Siskiwit Falls before emptying into Malone Bay.

On this narrow bridge of land between the lake and the bay is Malone Bay Campground, one of the most beautiful in the park. On the bayside there are smooth pebble beaches to comb and views of the long reefs that separate the bay from Lake Superior. The campground features five shelters, group and individual campsites, pit toilets, tables, a dock, and a ranger stationed there for the summer. Siskiwit Lake is known for its wide variety of sport fish, including brook trout and lake trout.

EAST CHICKENBONE TRAIL

Distance: 1.6 miles
High point: 720 feet
Hiking time: 1–2 hours
Rating: easy to moderate

The East Chickenbone Trail begins 0.5 miles from McCargoe Cove Campground and swings around the east end of Chickenbone Lake to the

Greenstone Ridge Trail. It is often combined with part of the Greenstone and Indian Portage trails for a pleasant 6.6-mile day hike around Chickenbone Lake from McCargoe Cove.

From the junction with Indian Portage Trail, this trail dips, crosses Chickenbone Creek on a wooden bridge, and then makes a steep climb out of the geologic fault trench. It follows the ridge top, dipping and climbing, before descending to a small pond.

The trail crosses this pond and then swings sharply to the east and follows the other side. The trail leaves the pond and swings south, where it crosses three small bogs before breaking out at the eastern edge of Chickenbone Lake. The trail skirts around the lake and then climbs a ridge to East Chickenbone Campground and the junction with the Greenstone Ridge Trail (see Chapter 6).

HATCHET LAKE TRAIL

Distance: 2.6 miles
High point: 1057 feet
Hiking time: 2–3 hours
Rating: moderate

This trail connects the Greenstone Ridge with the Minong Ridge and is used by many hikers out of Windigo who want to walk only a portion of the rugged Minong Ridge Trail. It is also the side trail to Hatchet Lake Campground for backpackers hiking along the Greenstone Ridge (see map on page 65).

From the ridge the trail descends sharply from its high point of 1057 feet until it nears the shore of Hatchet Lake, where it swings east. It passes the spur to the Hatchet Lake Campground (see Chapter 6), 0.3 miles from the Greenstone Ridge, and winds its way past the eastern end of the lake.

From here it swings north, crosses a stream, and then quickly arrives at a junction with a side trail to the patrol cabin on the north shore of the lake. It climbs a low ridge, passes a second junction to the patrol cabin 0.2 miles from the first junction, and levels out. The trail then begins to dip and climb as it drops off the ridge, crosses a second stream, and finally makes its ascent to the junction with the Minong Ridge Trail.

From here you can hike either to Todd Harbor (1.4 miles) or Little Todd Harbor (5.3 miles) for the night (see Chapter 7). Before embarking for Little Todd Harbor, keep in mind that the Minong Ridge Trail is rugged.

Even the short trails often lead into thick, canopied forests. (Photo by
Steve and Carol Maass)

10 THE SHORT TRAILS, EAST

*Tobin Harbor • Mount Franklin • Lane Cove • Daisy Farm
and Mount Ojibway • Stoll Loop • Lookout Louise • Mott
Island Circuit • Raspberry Island • Lighthouse Loop*

Some backpackers never leave the Rock Harbor area. They make their
way down the waterway, stopping for a couple of days at every campground. They explore only a limited section of the Island, but rarely run out
of places to hike or things to see.

The trails in and around Rock Harbor and the eastern end of the park
offer the most variety of any on Isle Royale. Not only do they range in difficulty, but their views and scenery vary from the bare crest of the
Greenstone Ridge to the panorama from Lookout Louise to the half-hidden
beaches and coves on Mott Island.

There are two scenic loops from the Rock Harbor Lodge that can be
turned into leisurely day hikes. For an afternoon of craggy coastline and
pounding Lake Superior surf there is the Stoll Trail Loop that travels east of
the lodge to the end of Scoville Point. To the west of the lodge you can
combine the Tobin Harbor Trail with a portion of Mount Franklin and Rock
Harbor trails for a 6.4-mile trek that rarely leaves the shoreline.

Much more rugged is the 5.1-mile loop along Daisy Farm, Mount Ojibway, and a portion of the Greenstone Ridge Trail. The walk involves climb-

ing several ridges, including the Greenstone, but the views from Mount Ojibway Lookout Tower are excellent. So are those from Mount Franklin, which can be seen on an overnight trek to Lane Cove Campground. This trip involves a one-way hike of 6.8 miles from Rock Harbor Lodge along the Mount Franklin and Lane Cove trails to the secluded Lane Cove campground.

One other option for those staying at Rock Harbor Lodge is to rent a canoe or rowboat at the camp store and combine paddling with hiking. With this water transportation, several days can be spent hiking Lookout Louise, Mott Island, Raspberry Island, or the Edisen Fishery Lighthouse Loop.

TOBIN HARBOR TRAIL

Distance: 3 miles
High point: 640 feet
Hiking time: 1–2 hours
Rating: easy

Although the trail rises and dips a little, it is a wide, dry, and easy path to hike. Many hikers view the Tobin Harbor Trail as a more scenic alternative to the stretch from Rock Harbor Lodge to Three-Mile Campground. It can be combined with the Rock Harbor Trail for a 6.6-mile day hike or can be shortened to 4.0 miles by cutting over at Suzy's Cave.

The trail begins near the seaplane dock on Tobin Harbor at the junction with the trail to Rock Harbor Lodge. From here, Tobin Harbor Trail gently rises west and passes an unmarked trail that leads back to group campsites in the Rock Harbor Campground. The trail continues to climb and dip

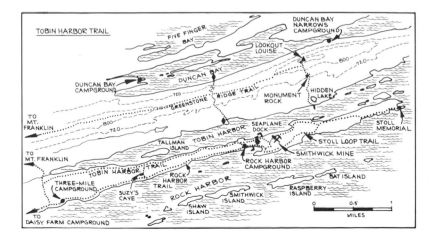

gently along the shoreline of the harbor and is a pleasure to hike: The ground is soft and well shaded by a thick canopy of birch, spruce, and fir. The views of the protected waterway and the small islands that dot it never go away.

The junction to Suzy's Cave is 1.8 miles from the seaplane dock. The cave, an inland sea arch created when Lake Superior was at a higher level, is a short climb away on the ridge. From the junction to the cave the trail levels out somewhat and follows the shoreline until it comes to the end of the harbor. From here it finally leaves the water, wanders 100 yards through the forest, and arrives at the junction with the Mount Franklin Trail.

At this point you can head north on the Mount Franklin Trail and reach the Greenstone Ridge Trail (1.5 miles) or hike south 0.5 miles and reach Three-Mile Campground on the Rock Harbor Trail.

MOUNT FRANKLIN TRAIL

Distance: 2.0 miles
High point: 1074 feet
Hiking time: 60-90 minutes
Rating: moderate

The Mount Franklin Trail is often the entry ramp for hikers tackling the Greenstone Ridge Trail. From a junction with the Rock Harbor Trail, it runs 2.0 miles to the ridge, passing the Tobin Harbor Trail along the way. Mount Franklin, with its incredible views, is actually a short climb east on the Greenstone Ridge Trail.

The Mount Franklin Trail begins 0.2 miles west of Three-Mile Campground, which you can hike or paddle to. The trail departs from the junction with the Rock Harbor Trail by immediately climbing a ridge and leveling off on top. The trail descends from the ridge, crosses a planked bog, and arrives in a valley where it junctions with the Tobin Harbor Trail, 0.5 miles from Three-Mile Campground. To the east on the Tobin Harbor Trail lies Suzy's Cave (1.2 miles) and the Rock Harbor seaplane dock (3.0 miles).

After the junction, the trail crosses the Tobin Creek swamp and then climbs a low ridge. From here it drops into another bog, crosses it, swinging west and following the north side of a dried-up marsh. Then the trail swings sharply north and begins its steep climb to the Greenstone Ridge. The hike to the junction of the Greenstone Trail is a knee-bender that lasts for 0.5 miles.

If you are heading for Lane Cove, stash your pack after reaching the junction and scramble west to the top of Mount Franklin. Officially, Mount Franklin Trail ends here and becomes the Lane Cove Trail, which winds 2.3 miles to the secluded Lane Cove Campground. West on the Greenstone is Mount Ojibway (2.8 miles); the junction of the trail to Lookout Louise is 4.8 miles east.

LANE COVE TRAIL

Distance: 2.3 miles
High point: 1074 feet
Hiking time: 2–3 hours
Rating: moderate to difficult

The Lane Cove Campground was moved farther west in 1983, making the trail almost 0.5 miles shorter than indicated in old park literature and on signposts.

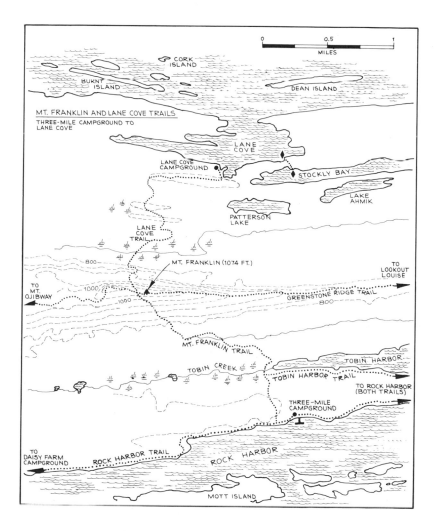

Lane Cove Trail begins with an immediate and steep descent of the Greenstone Ridge, using two series of switchbacks to climb down off the Island's backbone. At the base of the ridge the trail crosses two ponds and then begins to climb up and over a series of low ridges.

Eventually, it arrives and follows an old bog, crosses it at one end, and climbs one more ridge. What you are hiking along now is really a 3000-year old beach line of Lake Superior. From the ridge the trail descends to the cove at the shoreline.

At a junction near the shoreline, the trail to the west leads off a short distance to the campground.

The campground, a pleasant area, offers only individual campsites. But there are pit toilets and a large number of bugs from mid-June to late July. The mosquitoes can be a pain at times, especially when you are trying to eat, but the area is beautiful and well worth a little extra bug dope in the hair. This is one of the few campgrounds where you can view Canada from your tent site.

DAISY FARM AND MOUNT OJIBWAY TRAILS

Distance: 5.1 miles
High point: 1136 feet
Hiking time: 3-5 hours
Rating: moderate

For those hiking the loop from Daisy Farm Campground, it is easier to hike clockwise by first walking the Daisy Farm Trail, which reaches the Greenstone Ridge at one of the ridge's lowest points. Most hikers, eager to see the views from the lookout tower, immediately tackle the steeper Mount Ojibway Trail.

From the Daisy Farm Campground the 1.7-mile Mount Ojibway Trail gently climbs to the top of Ransom Hill. It moves through spruce–fir forest, passes an open meadow with scattered white pines, and finally peaks at the top of the hill. The trail descends along the north slope of Ransom Hill through paper-birch forest before leveling out and crossing a bog created by Tobin Creek, 0.9 miles north of Daisy Farm.

The trail climbs a second ridge and levels out at the top. At one point it's possible to see the Ojibway Lookout Tower to the north on the Greenstone Ridge. The trail descends again and then makes its final assault up the Greenstone Ridge. Portions of the climb can be steep. But halfway up, the trees thin out and you are rewarded with views of the south shore.

The trail ends at the lookout tower, where there are splendid views of both shores of the Island. Next to the tower is the junction with the Greenstone Ridge Trail (see Chapter 6). From this point the junction of the Mount Franklin Trail lies 2.8 miles to the east; West Chickenbone is 7.5 miles to the west.

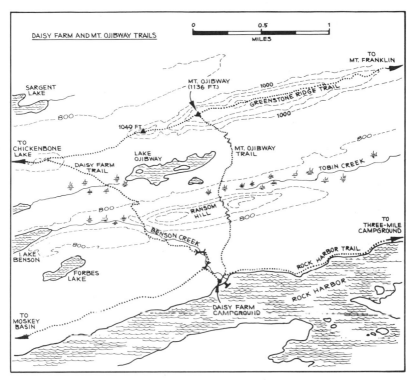

Greenstone Ridge to Daisy Farm

Distance: 1.9 miles

Daisy Farm Trail arrives at the Greenstone Ridge at a relatively low point, making it one of the easiest routes to the ridge. The path begins from the junction with the Greenstone Ridge Trail 1.5 miles west of the Mount Ojibway Lookout Tower.

From here it gently descends off the ridge for 0.5 miles until it arrives at a low, wet area where the stream to Angleworm Lake begins. Beaver have dammed this portion and created a small pond. The trail departs from the pond and climbs over a low ridge to planked swamp. Swamp vegetation such as bog laurel, labrador tea, black spruce, and tamarack can be spotted in this area.

The trail leaves the swamp, climbs over the western tip of Ransom Hill, and crosses Benson Creek about 1.0 miles from Daisy Farm Campground. The trail follows the western side of the creek—one known for its brook trout—crosses to the other side and back on two bridges, and arrives at the junction with the Rock Harbor Trail to Moskey Basin.

From the junction the trail winds into Daisy Farm Campground, one of the largest on the Island (see Chapter 7).

STOLL LOOP TRAIL

Distance: 4.3 miles round trip
High point: 639 feet
Walking time: 1½ – 2½ hours
Rating: easy   Map: page 95

This easy looped trail begins at Rock Harbor Lodge and travels 2.0 miles east to rugged Scoville Point. The trail winds back and forth between the forest and the shoreline, where craggy bluffs and sharp cliffs are testimony to Lake Superior's power and persistent erosion.

Stoll Trail begins near the dining room and lodge units. The trail wanders through the forest for 0.25 miles, with brief glimpses of Rock Harbor before breaking out on a high bluff overlooking the last few islands that form the harbor. An exhibit describing the ancient copper pit is nearby, 0.7 miles from the lodge, with several pits visible.

Just past the exhibit is a junction of a side trail that intersects the return loop on the Tobin Harbor. Stoll Trail continues east, stays near the shoreline for another 0.7 miles, passes scenic views of the rugged bluffs and cliffs on the Lake Superior shoreline, and finally reaches the rocky end of Scoville Point. At the tip of the point is a memorial to Albert Stoll, Jr., the Detroit *News* reporter who campaigned to turn Isle Royale into a national park.

Indian copper mine pit near Stoll Trail.

From Scoville Point you backtrack 0.6 miles to where the return loop trail divides. It hugs Tobin Harbor back to Rock Harbor Lodge. All along the way are good views of the harbor. The remains of Smithwick Mine can also be seen, right before the trail reaches the lodge.

LOOKOUT LOUISE TRAIL

Distance: 1 mile
High point: 880 feet
Walking time: 45–60 minutes
Rating: difficult   **Map: page 95**

By renting a canoe at Rock Harbor Lodge, you can combine paddling with hiking and visit some of the most interesting spots on the Island. One of them is Lookout Louise, a favorite with visitors. The lookout spot provides the most spectacular view in the park, but the 1.0-mile trail is a straight, uphill climb.

The easiest way to reach the trail head is to rent a canoe and launch it from the seaplane dock. From here you paddle across Tobin Harbor and then follow the shoreline east for about 1.0 miles to the Hidden Lake dock. The trail departs from the dock and winds around Hidden Lake. Keep your eyes open around this small lake, because moose often visit its mineral licks.

A half-mile up, the trail passes Monument Rock, a high stone pinnacle carved by Lake Superior waves when that body of water was at a higher elevation. A little farther on and the trail arrives at the junction with the start of the Greenstone Ridge Trail.

From here it is a 0.1-mile climb to Lookout Louise. From the summit you can see Duncan and Five Finger Bay and the Canadian mainland 20 miles to the north. This scene probably ends up in more home movies than any other in the park.

MOTT ISLAND CIRCUIT TRAIL

Distance: 2.6 miles
High point: 640 feet
Walking time: 1–2 hours
Rating: easy

A full day can be spent paddling from Rock Harbor Lodge to Mott Island and hiking the beautiful and little-used Mott Island Circuit Trail (see map on page 78). The paddle is about 4.0 miles from Rock Harbor, and in good weather conditions you can plan on 2–3 hours each way.

Mott Island is the site of park headquarters and is a bustling place during the summer, as rangers, maintenance people, and trail crews pass

Old Rock Harbor Lighthouse, off Old Lighthouse Trail.

through. Don't land your canoe at the main dock. Paddle to the beach on the east side of the harbor and secure your boat there.

The circular trail begins and ends near the airplane dock. By staying to the left, the trail follows the protected shore of Rock Harbor, rising and dipping gently. It stays in the forest for the first 1.0 miles, with only quick views of the water through the trees before passing the cove where the NPS docks its supply barges.

From here the trail hugs the coast and winds through a handful of small coves with views of the harbor and nearby islands. At one point it dips down to a pebbled cove at the northeast tip of Mott Island, where you can see Lorelei Lane—the narrow channel that divides the outer islands to the east.

At this point the trail swings east and follows the Lake Superior shoreline, passing more little coves. If the afternoon is sunny, you can sunbathe on the smooth, bare rocks along the shore. Eventually, the trail swings back to its beginning near the airplane dock.

RASPBERRY ISLAND TRAIL

Distance: 0.8 miles
High point: 646 feet
Walking time: 30 minutes
Rating: easy

LIGHTHOUSE TRAIL LOOP

Distance: 0.4 miles
High point: 640 feet
Walking time: 15 minutes
Rating: easy

These two spots are not really hiking trails but are interesting places to visit. Raspberry Island is directly across Rock Harbor Lodge and is an easy paddle on a calm day (see map on page 76). The self-guiding trail has interpretive markers that point out the unusual plants and other features of this excellent little bog.

Across from Daisy Farm Campground is the Edisen Fishery and the 0.5-mile loop to the old Rock Harbor Lighthouse (see map on page 78). This well-preserved fishery was operated by Pete Edisen for more than 50 years. From the fishery begins the short trail that winds to the lighthouse. En route it passes the burial site of an Island miner.

The lighthouse was built in 1855 to help guide boats into the harbor during the mining era. Later, visitors used it as a summer home. The NPS began to stabilize the abandoned structure in 1962. The return loop departs from the lighthouse, follows the cliffs overlooking Middle Islands Passage, and returns to the fishery.

For those who don't want to paddle to Raspberry Island or the Rock Harbor Lighthouse, the park concessioner offers guided day trips to both spots.

Attwood Beach on the South Shore.

PART THREE

ISLE ROYALE BY PADDLE

11 THE INLAND LAKES, NORTH

Rock Harbor • Lake Richie • Lake LeSage •
Lake Livermore • Chickenbone Lake • McCargoe Cove

Distance: 20 miles (Rock Harbor to McCargoe Cove)
Portages: 5
Longest portage: 2.2 miles
Paddling time: 2-3 days

There may be 170 miles of footpaths, but for some backpackers each summer Isle Royale is a paddler's park. Paddling allows you to cover more area, carry more gear, and, from the seat of a canoe in the middle of a lake, gives you a clear and different view of the Island. Plus it's easier—even with the portages—and there are fewer insects out on the water.

The disadvantages of choosing the boat over the boot is that you must have a canoe or kayak and pay an additional charge for ferrying it to the park and back. And it's possible you may be holed up somewhere because of foul weather and rough water. No matter how hard it rains, on foot you can always pack up and hike out—not true when paddling.

But the key difference for many is that more often than not paddling is

Chickenbone Lake from Greenstone Ridge.

the only way to seek out the park's isolated corners. And that type of experience is priceless in today's standing-room-only world.

The water routes of Isle Royale are not difficult. Most are well protected and are strung together by short, though not-always-level, portages. Backpackers interested in paddling must have previous canoeing or kayaking experience. This is no place to learn how to handle a boat. But with the right preparation, equipment, and route, the Island can be your first extended water trip.

Almost all paddlers arrive at Rock Harbor because Windigo offers limited travel. The most common trip is to paddle Rock Harbor and then cut across the park through the northern inland lakes of Richie, LeSage, Livermore, and Chickenbone to McCargoe Cove. Once in McCargoe you can weave your way through the bay and coves of the Five Fingers to circle back to Rock Harbor. The trip takes 6–7 days at a comfortable pace.

Always keep an eye out for the water markers placed around the park to assist paddlers. There are two kinds. *Portage markers* are long rectangular signs pointed at the top, stained dark redwood around the outside, and have a large *p* in the middle. *Canoe campground markers* are similar, except that they display a tent instead of a *p*.

ROCK HARBOR

If the Greenstone Ridge Trail is the boulevard of footpaths, then Rock Harbor is its counterpart when it comes to the Island's waterways. The long narrow harbor, which stretches 9.5 miles from Rock Harbor Lodge to Moskey Basin, is a busy sea-lane during the summer. Everything from *Ranger III* to sailboats and ranger patrol boats can be seen zipping up and down the channel.

It is also the first stretch for most paddlers and a good place to start. The outer islands that form the barrier in front of Lake Superior break up the lake's large, slow-rolling swells and make the harbor calm most of the time. Even if the weather is stormy and Rock Harbor becomes choppy, there are five campgrounds along its shoreline and almost an endless number of coves and inlets to wait out the rough water.

Directly across from Rock Harbor Lodge is Raspberry Island (map on page 78) with its short nature walk (see Chapter 10); Tookers Island Campground is 1.5 miles west. This boaters' campground has two shelters, pit toilets, a dock, and a scenic cove nearby. But being close to Rock Harbor Lodge, it is often filled with powerboaters.

If conditions are calm, kayakers can weave their way along the outer islands, passing through narrow gaps and channels. Park rangers strongly recommend that canoeists stay near the main shoreline and away from open water of Lake Superior as much as possible.

Mott Island is 4.0 miles from Rock Harbor and is the site of the NPS park headquarters, a scenic 2.6-mile circular trail (see Chapter 10), but no campground. Another 1.5 miles west of Mott Island is Caribou Island Campground, on the very western tip of West Caribou Island. This camping spot is a pleasant area, with two shelters, dock, and pit toilets.

Right across from each other in Rock Harbor are Daisy Farm Campground (see Chapter 7) and the historic Edisen Fishery (see Chapter 10 and map on page 78), both about 6.5 miles from the lodge. Near here the harbor narrows into Moskey Basin. Three miles west of Daisy Farm, an easy 1½-hour paddle away, is Moskey Basin Campground.

Moskey Basin is the point when many canoeists and kayakers make their first portage, carrying their boats over the 2.2-mile distance from the campground along the Lake Richie Trail to the first inland lake. The route is not difficult but does wind over two small ridges before reaching the water (for a trail description, see Chapter 7).

LAKE RICHIE

Lake Richie is a favorite among paddlers and is an ideal place to spend an extra day. The main body of the lake is broken up by four islands, the largest being Hastings Island, and two arms extend along the western shoreline. The lower arm extends 0.75 miles and is the beginning of the portage trail to Chippewa Harbor (see map on page 120).

The upper arm extends northwest almost 1.0 miles. On the western side of the arm is the marker for the Intermediate Lake portage; on the eastern side is Lake Richie Canoe Campground, situated on a bluff with a nice view of the surrounding area. The Lake Richie Campground is on the eastern side, 0.2 miles from the junction of the Lake Richie and Indian Portage trails (see Chapter 9).

The lake is a hot spot for pike fishing. All along the shore or between the islands are marshes and weed beds where hard-fighting fish might be found. For better results, paddlers can seek out sections of the lake that see little action from shore fishermen. Although that might be any part of the western side of the lake, the traditional good spots are the small channels between the islands and the weed beds along the east shore of the lower arm.

Lake Richie to Lake LeSage Portage

Rating: difficult
Distance: 0.6 miles

The portage is marked and located on the north shore, directly across from Hastings Island (see map on page 87). The route is short but steep: It begins at the shoreline and climbs 100 feet before leveling off on a ridge. The trail then descends to the junction with the Indian Portage Trail around Lake LeSage. Paddlers continue straight ahead, climb another small ridge, and then drop to the Lake LeSage shoreline.

LAKE LeSAGE

Lake LeSage is more like two narrow lakes situated side-by-side and connected by a small channel. They are divided by two long peninsulas that jut out in the middle. The portage from Lake Richie leaves you in the middle of Lake LeSage's southern half, and it takes about 15 minutes to cross through the channel to the next portage on the northern half.

Or you could take your time and stop for lunch at the tip of the western peninsula. It's a great picnic area, and you can easily beach your canoe or kayak on the small rocky point of land. The channel between the two halves of the lake is also the best place to hook a northern pike or yellow perch. Another fishing spot is near the small island on the south side of the western peninsula.

Lake LeSage to Lake Livermore Portage

Rating: moderate
Distance: 0.5 miles

The portage is at the northwest corner of the upper half of LeSage and might be difficult to see at first (see map on page 91). The trail is short but, like the portage from Lake Richie, steep in places.

It departs from Lake LeSage and gradually climbs a ridge before leveling out on top. From the top of the ridge to Lake Livermore the trail descends

Northern pike catch, Lake Richie.

so sharply that you might end up bouncing the back of the boat off the ground. The trail arrives at the southwest corner of Lake Livermore.

LAKE LIVERMORE

The long narrow lake doesn't have the outstanding fishing as those on either side of it. The weed beds are not as extensive nor do the northern pike seem as big. There are quite a few beaver lodges around it, and they are interesting to paddle past.

Lake Livermore to Chickenbone Lake Portage

Rating: easy
Distance: 0.2 miles

This very short portage climbs a little to a low point on the Greenstone Ridge Trail. At this point the portage passes a serene little waterfall formed by the creek flowing between the two lakes. The portage then dips down to Chickenbone Lake in the middle of the lower arm.

CHICKENBONE LAKE

The V-shaped lake is another delightful place to paddle or spend an extra day resting up. The lower arm is about 1.7 miles in length, and at its western end is West Chickenbone Campground (see Chapter 6), a favorite among campers. The upper arm is about 0.75 miles long and heads northeast toward McCargoe Cove.

Wildlife is plentiful around the lake. It is usually possible to spot beavers, loons, and moose feeding along the shoreline. The best way to observe the wildlife is to paddle along the shore at dusk.

Chickenbone also has excellent fishing for pike, perch, and, if you are skillful enough, walleye. One of the best places to cast a lure is the eastern end of the lower arm. The weed beds around the three small islands in the middle are especially productive for pike and perch.

Chickenbone Lake to McCargoe Cove Portage

Rating: moderate to difficult
Distance: 1 mile   **Map: page 88**

A portage marker is on the very end of the upper arm of Chickenbone Lake. The trail (described in Chapter 9) is a hilly climb on the ridge along Chickenbone Creek. There are three steep ascents up the ridge before reaching McCargoe Cove Campground. The last one can be skipped, however, by putting-in where the trail passes an open, sandy area. At this point the stream is deep and wide enough to paddle the rest of the way into McCargoe Cove and the dock at the campground.

McCARGOE COVE

This stunning body of water flows from Chickenbone Creek northeast to Lake Superior. The campground (see Chapter 7) is one of the nicest in the park, and the paddle along this waterway is the highpoint of many trips.

Bluffs enclose McCargoe, but its shore is broken up by a handful of coves and inlets tempting to the fisherman. It is 2.0 miles from the campground to Birch Island, near the mouth of the cove. There is a small boater campground on the island, which includes a shelter, table, and grill.

Birch Island blocks the entrance to Brady Cove, a secluded little body of water off to the east of McCargoe. This cove is an excellent place to land a pike. It is also the traditional spot for paddlers to stay and wait for rough water to subside before venturing into Lake Superior.

From Birch Island and Brady Cove you can paddle around Indian Point into the open waters of Lake Superior to the Five Fingers area at the park's eastern end. Extreme caution has to be used in this section, because the lake can develop slow rollers that sweep to the north side of the Island. In storms, the north shore is notorious for being the roughest section of the park.

Isolated islands dot the shore of the Five Fingers region of the park.

12 THE FIVE FINGERS

Herring Bay, Pickerel Cove, Robinson Bay • Amygdaloid Channel, Crystal Cove, Belle Harbor • Stockly Bay, Five Finger Bay, Duncan Bay • Merritt Lane, Tobin Harbor

Distance: 13.5 miles (McCargoe Cove to Rock Harbor)
Portages: 5
Longest portage: 0.8 miles
Paddling time: 2–3 days

At the east end of the Island is a collection of long, narrow channels, fiord-like harbors, and secluded coves and inlets loved by all who pass through. They are known as the Five Fingers. Isle Royale is a beautiful place, but the Five Fingers are the diamonds at the end of the pendant.

These long, steep ridges that reach into the lake offer rugged beauty, calm water, and visual links to the Island's past. You could easily spend a week or even two exploring this area that covers the far eastern portion of the park and seven campgrounds.

Canoes and kayaks are well suited for the Five Fingers. The Lane Cove Trail is the lone footpath into the heart of the east end. Powerboaters can travel through much of the Five Fingers but have only four campgrounds with deep-water docks. Paddlers, on the other hand, find calm water, narrow gaps between islands to squeeze through, and a handful of old cabins and camps to explore.

Plan at least 3 days to paddle from McCargoe Cove to Rock Harbor, spending the first night either at Pickerel Cove or Belle Isle and the second at one of the two campgrounds in Duncan Bay. You can cover this stretch in less time but will be disappointed at the end for not having scheduled additional days.

Also remember that Belle Isle, the two campgrounds in Duncan Bay, and the one in Merritt Lane are popular havens for powerboaters. It is inevitable that you will hear the roar of their engines in these areas or be crowded out of the shelters.

HERRING BAY, PICKEREL COVE, AND ROBINSON BAY

Park officials are considering a 1.0-mile portage trail from Brady Cove to Pickerel Cove (next to Herring Bay) so paddlers can avoid the brief encounter with open water from the mouth of McCargoe Cove to Herring Bay. That route, in which you round Indian Point and paddle for 1.5 miles to Herring Bay, is presently the only way to reach Pickerel Cove from the west.

Old fish camp on Johnson Island, Five Fingers region.

Canoeists should use extreme caution and wait for good weather when entering this stretch of Lake Superior. Even on calm days, slow rollers can develop along the north shore of Isle Royale for an extremely difficult paddle in an open canoe.

Kayakers with skirts, however, have less to worry about and will thoroughly enjoy this stint with Lake Superior. The stretch from McCargoe Cove to Herring Bay is scenic, with grand views of the west end of Amygdaloid Island, the rugged north shore, and mainland Canada off in the distance. There is also something exciting and awe inspiring about paddling in Lake Superior. Maybe it's the notion that the lake is the largest body of freshwater in the world; or its long history of shipwrecks, of which more than 20 are near the Island. Whatever, the short paddle is bound to leave goosebumps on the back of your neck.

By cutting across the mouth of Herring Bay to Amygdaloid Island you reach the North Shore Ranger Station where park personnel are stationed all summer. Most paddlers choose to enter Herring Bay and make their way to its longest inlet in the southeast corner. Tucked away about halfway along the south shore of the inlet is the portage marker to Pickerel Cove.

Herring Bay to Pickerel Cove Portage

Rating: easy
Distance: 0.1 miles

The hop-skip-and-jump between Herring Bay and Pickerel Cove is the shortest and sweetest portage in the park. The trail is historical: It was originally used to roll herring barrels to waiting cargo ships in Herring Bay.

The portage takes you to a spot deep inside the beautiful cove. The long, narrow body of water is stunning and usually bustling with waterfowl. Right to the east of the portage is Pickerel Cove Canoe Campground. The little campground, with flat space for only a few tents, is on the ridge overlooking the cove. There are no pit toilets, but the view is great and there are large, flat rocks nearby—ideal for lying out in the sun. Although Pickerel Cove is only a short paddle from McCargoe Cove, most canoeists prefer it over Belle Isle because of its isolation.

Once in Pickerel Cove you could paddle the south shore all the way to Lane Cove or cut through the first gap along the north side. The gap separates the peninsula on the mainland from Horner Island. On the other side of this channel is Robinson Bay, which extends for another 2.0 miles to the west. To the east is a narrow channel that leads to Belle Harbor.

Or you could paddle straight across Robinson Bay where you would find a very small opening between two islands. A flat-bottomed kayak might be able to squeeze through or, possibly, a light canoe. But there are only inches of water, and overloaded parties will have to get out and carry their boats a few yards across the opening.

On the other side of the opening is a second narrow channel between Robinson Bay and Belle Harbor and still another narrow gap almost straight ahead. This one is wider and deeper because it separates the peninsula on the mainland from Belle Isle. On the other side of the opening is Amygdaloid Channel, a wider and more open waterway than Pickerel Cove or Robinson Bay.

AMYGDALOID CHANNEL, CRYSTAL COVE, AND BELLE HARBOR

Two miles west of the gap between Robinson Island and Amygdaloid Channel is the NPS ranger station. To the east of the gap, 1.5 miles away, is Crystal Cove, which marks the eastern end of Amygdaloid.

Crystal Cove is the fishery of Milford and Myrtle Johnson and includes a handful of cabins, docks, and fish-drying racks. Milford arrived on the Island in 1906 and until his death, spent most of his summers fishing in the park for lake trout, white fish, and herring. Today, Myrtle holds one of the few permits to fish commercially at Isle Royale. A family assists her with the fishing during the summer, with much of the catch sold to the Rock Harbor Lodge. From Crystal Cove you sprint across Amygdaloid Channel in 15 or 20 minutes to Belle Isle Campground, which features, among other things, an outdoor grill and covered picnic area. Belle Isle Campground is another scenic and historical spot. The campground was the site of a large resort in the 1920s that catered to the grand lake steamers of the time. Still visible are the cement slabs that were shuffleboard courts, and the pilings of the original dock across from the campground on Belle Harbor, near the present dock.

Along with the grill and picnic area, Belle Isle has six shelters, individual campsites, pit toilets, and tables. The sunrise on a clear morning is especially stunning from this campground.

The islands east of Belle Isle—Captain Kidd, Green, and Dean—can be

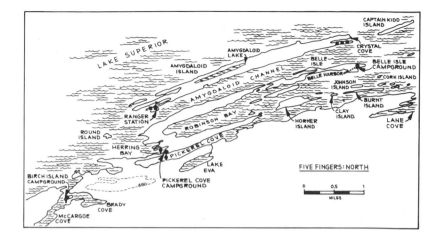

visited but caution should be used in paddling this area. It has little protection from Lake Superior and can turn suddenly rough. South of the campground dock is another set of islands that harbor several old fishing camps. Almost straight across is Johnson Island and its old fishing camp and boat houses. The cabin in the camp is still being used and should not be disturbed. There is a lone cabin on Clay Island, and the north shore of Horner Island also once supported a small camp.

Southeast from Belle Isle is Lane Cove, about an hour's paddle away. The stretch between the two is exposed to Lake Superior and can be choppy. After entering the mouth to Lane Cove the portage marker will be visible to your left, in the southeast corner. The campground in Lane Cove (see Chapter 10) is very scenic but usually has more than its share of bugs.

Lane Cove to Stockly Bay Portage

Rating: easy
Distance: 0.1 miles

This portage comes in a close second with the one at Pickerel Cove as the easiest crossing in the park. Among the trees east of the trail was the site of the old Lane Cove Campground. The portage arrives at the western end of Stockly Bay.

STOCKLY BAY, FIVE FINGER BAY, AND DUNCAN BAY

Stockly Bay is a long, narrow waterway that extends 1.5 miles northeast into Five Finger Bay. It is well protected and so is much of Five Finger Bay. But once you venture past the islands in the middle of the bay toward the

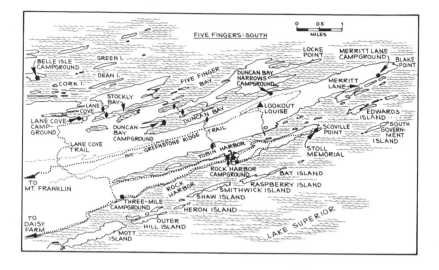

mouth, the water can be unstable.

By following the south shore of Stockly Bay, you will enter the western edge of Five Finger Bay, round one point, and paddle past an inlet to the west. After you shoot across this inlet and round a second point, you will enter a longer inlet. Head west and look to the south to spot the portage marker to Duncan Bay.

Five Finger Bay to Duncan Bay Portage

Rating: easy
Distance: 0.2 miles

This portage is twice as long as the last two and involves a little more climbing. Still, it is nothing to sweat over. On the other side you will come out on Duncan Bay, across from the western end of its largest Island. Duncan Bay Campground is a 15-20-minute paddle to the southwest.

The campground is at the end of a peninsula that juts out in the middle of the bay. It is a nice place to spend an extra day, especially if you secured one of the two shelters that overlook the water. There is also an individual campsite, tables, grills, and a dock. Nearby is a small bluff that leads to a good view of the western end of the bay.

Duncan Bay, with its many islands and coves, is noted for its fine pike fishing. It takes 1½-2 hours to paddle east to Duncan Bay Narrows and the campground there. Although not as scenic as the other, Duncan Bay Narrows Campground is a pleasant place with two shelters, tables, grill, and pit toilets. Both of them are popular among powerboaters.

From Duncan Bay you can either round Blake Point, a very risky stretch of water, or portage into Tobin Harbor. All canoeists should portage into

Tobin Harbor. Blake Point, the eastern tip of the Island, is notorious for being rough, choppy, and unsuitable for small craft. For a 2.5-mile stretch, from the mouth of Duncan Bay until you round the point to Merritt Lane, you will be paddling in open Lake Superior with nothing breaking the surf. The shoreline around Blake Point is composed of steep cliffs with no place to beach.

Duncan Bay to Tobin Harbor Portage

Rating: extremely difficult
Distance: 0.8 miles

The alternative to paddling Blake Point is safer but no more easy on the back. The 0.8-mile portage is by far the worst in the park. From the shoreline of Duncan Bay to the shoreline of Tobin Harbor, the trail rises 175 feet and then drops back down.

In Duncan Bay, the portage is on the south shore about one-third of the way to Duncan Bay Narrows Campground. The first 0.25 miles is a back-breaking climb along switchbacks to the top of the Greenstone Ridge. This is the steepest part and can be endured only by taking your time and stopping for many breaks.

Eventually, the trail levels out at the top of the ridge and meets the Greenstone Ridge Trail. From here the trail descends the ridge to Tobin Harbor at a more gradual rate than before. In Tobin Harbor, you will be just northwest of the seaplane dock across the water.

MERRITT LANE AND TOBIN HARBOR

Those who endure the steep portage shouldn't rush across Tobin Harbor just to invade the camp store. Tobin Harbor and Merritt Lane are another scenic part of the Island worth spending the extra time to see.

Calm water is met almost immediately after rounding Blake Point. One-half mile from the tip is Merritt Lane Campground, a small site with one shelter, one campsite, a dock, a pit toilet, and not much flat land. Don't be disappointed if a fishing party has taken over the place.

From here the paddling becomes interesting because there is a group of islands, coves, and channels you can explore just west of the campground. Eventually you paddle into an open area where you will be able to view Scoville Point and the mouth of Tobin Harbor.

It is safer to paddle straight into Tobin Harbor to reach Rock Harbor Lodge rather than trying to round Scoville Point. The stretch from the point to Raspberry Island can be considerably rougher than Tobin Harbor.

The mouth of the harbor is partially blocked by several islands, and a dozen cabins are scattered along the shoreline. These are the summer homes of life-time residents, and most of them were built before the Island became a national park.

Sunset paddle, Tobin Harbor.

Paddlers who arrive at Merritt Lane Campground and find it filled need not panic. It is only another 4.0 miles to Rock Harbor Lodge by way of Tobin Harbor.

Tobin Harbor to Rock Harbor Portage

Rating: easy
Distance: 0.2 miles

As paddlers arrive at the seaplane dock in Tobin Harbor, the last thing on their minds is the portage through Rock Harbor Lodge to the *Ranger III* dock—the final portage before loading the boat on the ferry for the mainland. The walk from Tobin Harbor to Rock Harbor is easy and can be heroic: Curious lodge visitors, most of whom have rarely ventured beyond Rock Harbor Lodge and the nice park hotel, are intrigued and quick to inquire about someone carrying a boat on top of their head.

It is wise to stake out a shelter or campsite in Rock Harbor Lodge before pirating the camp store.

13 THE INLAND LAKES, SOUTH

Chippewa Harbor • Lake Whittlesey •
Wood Lake • Siskiwit Lake • Intermediate Lake

Distance: 18 miles (Lake Richie to Siskiwit Lake and back)
Portages: 5
Longest portage: 0.8 miles
Paddling time: 3-4 days

The southern inland lakes are a breed apart from the rest of the park. Most are accessible only to canoeists and kayakers. They require more time and energy to reach than those north of them. They are scenic but do not possess the overwhelming beauty of the Five Fingers.

They do offer one opportunity not found when hiking the Greenstone Ridge Trail or paddling through Rock Harbor. If you have the time and the shoulders willing to carry your boat, you can lose yourself for days at a time in this section of the park. Except for the south shore, nowhere else on the Island is such isolation possible.

Beginning with Lake Whittlesey and continuing with Wood Lake, Intermediate Lake, and most of Siskiwit Lake, this is a paddler's domain. The small number of backpackers who bring a boat to the park ensure that this section, even during the busiest week of the summer, will always retain its solitude.

The conventional way to reach this area is to paddle Rock Harbor and portage into Lake Richie (see maps on pages 76, 78 and 79). From here you paddle to the lower arm of the lake and endure a second long portage to Chippewa Harbor. After paddling and portaging through Lake Whittlesey, Wood Lake, and Siskiwit Lake, the loop is completed by doubling back through Intermediate Lake, Lake Richie, and Rock Harbor. The trip takes 8-10 days to complete. Anything less turns it into a canoe race.

The alternative is to hop on *Voyageur* and be dropped off at Chippewa Harbor or Malone Bay Campground. This reduces the trip back to Rock Harbor Lodge by 2-4 days. When beginning at Malone Bay, most paddlers choose the more scenic Wood Lake and Lake Whittlesey over the Intermediate Lake route back to Richie.

CHIPPEWA HARBOR

From Lake Richie paddle south to the end of the lower arm. While moving through this part of Lake Richie, anglers will want to keep their poles handy because this is an excellent area for pike. At the end of the arm is a portage marker and the mouth of a stream jammed with logs.

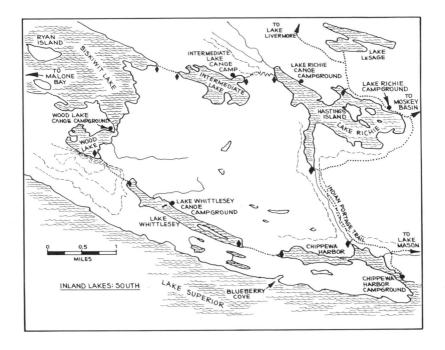

For those thinking they might skip the portage and try to paddle down the stream to Chippewa Harbor—don't. Although you could portage your boat around the log jam at the mouth of the stream, the trip would be one frustrating beaver dam after another until you give up and haul your boat up the ridge to the trail.

Lake Richie to Chippewa Harbor Portage

Rating: difficult
Distance: 0.8 miles

This portage is difficult and long. It follows the ravine the stream cut from Lake Richie to Chippewa Harbor, climbs up and over two high points on the ridge, and ascends 140 feet from its original elevation (for a complete trail description see Chapter 9). There is little you can do to make it easier except to plan on spending an entire day moving camp from Lake Richie to Chippewa Harbor.

The put-in is at the south end of the stream, now a wide and navigable waterway for canoeists or kayakers. A short paddle away you enter Chippewa Harbor, a beautiful sight for anybody who has just struggled over the trail with their boat. The water is well protected, and a paddle through the harbor is usually leisurely.

The harbor was the site of one of the Island's largest fishing camps in the early 1900s; several families built cabins and stayed year 'round. At one time there was even a small schoolhouse for the children. You can still see the remains of one boat as you paddle from the stream south to the Chippewa Harbor Campground. The boat, situated along the shoreline, will be to your left (to the east) just after you enter the harbor.

The campground (see Chapter 9) is pleasant because it sits on a bluff overlooking the harbor and its rugged opening to Lake Superior. Fishermen can try their luck for pike in any of the many coves and weed beds along the shore. The best spots tend to be deep in the harbor once you pass the narrows heading west.

From the Chippewa Harbor Campground you paddle back toward the stream to Lake Richie and then make a sharp turn west through the narrows and emerge in another long body of water. The whole area is scenic and this paddle is a favorite among canoeists and kayakers. Once in the second half of Chippewa Harbor, paddle to the west end and look for the portage marker in the southwest corner.

Chippewa Harbor to Lake Whittlesey Portage

Rating: moderate
Distance: 0.6 miles

The Chippewa Harbor end of the portage looks like it might have been used for hundreds of years by canoeists. Its mouth is carved out of sheer rock and narrows to a sharp *V*, as if an endless number of birch-bark and fiberglass boats have snuggled into it.

The trail is well marked and not difficult but does involve a little climbing with your boat. It leaves Chippewa Harbor and climbs a ridge. After leveling out on the ridge, the trail descends and climbs a second ridge. From the second ridge the trail swings more to the west and dips down to the shore of Lake Whittlesey.

LAKE WHITTLESEY

Lake Whittlesey is a narrow body of water that stretches almost 2.0 miles and is broken up at the east end by a pencil-thin island. Here, more than anywhere else, the isolation of Isle Royale is felt.

Anglers will find the lake a delight—northern pike thrive here. The small coves and weed beds around the island and across from it along the shore, tend to be the most productive. Whittlesey, however, is known for its walleye population, a fish that challenges the most skillful fisherman (see Chapter 3).

Many maps show the Lake Whittlesey Canoe Campground on the north shore across from the western end of the long island. The campground has been moved and is now another 0.5 miles west on the north shore, almost directly across from a pair of small islands. There is a pit toilet at the rear of the campground and sites for four tents. From the middle of the lake the campground can be spotted by looking for a canoe campground marker.

Lake Whittlesey to Wood Lake Portage

Rating: moderate
Distance: 0.6 miles

From the campground, paddle another 0.75 miles to the end of the lake as it curves slightly to the northwest. Here you will spot the portage marker for the 0.5-mile trail to Wood Lake. The trail is easier than the one from Chippewa Harbor: It climbs only 80 feet. There are some wet sections to watch for, especially after a rainfall.

The steepest part of the trail is at the beginning as you carry your boat from the waters of Lake Whittlesey 20 yards up to the top of a ridge. Before continuing inland, turn around at the top for a grand, final view of Whittlesey.

The trail follows the ridge, dips and climbs a little, and passes a high point that is clear of trees. From here it begins to descend to Wood Lake, passing through some wet areas along the way.

WOOD LAKE

The portage trail emerges at the southeast corner of Wood Lake, a small but delightful place to spend a day. The lake is about 0.5 miles wide along the south shore and tapers off to a narrow gap at the north end, which leads into Siskiwit Lake. A handful of small islands combine with many small coves to make the area another excellent place to fish for northern pike.

Paddle north to where the lake narrows and begins to flow into Siskiwit and look to the west for the marker to Wood Lake Canoe Campground. This spot provides ideal conditions for a wilderness campground because it has spaces for a handful of tents and is above the shoreline for a nice view of the lake. Directly across from the campground is a small cove where more than one pike has been landed.

By scrambling up and over the ridge behind the campsite, you arrive on the other side of the peninsula that separates the two lakes. The views from this spot are among the best in the park, because you can survey the eastern half of the Island's largest lake and the Greenstone Ridge off in the distance.

SISKIWIT LAKE

At a length of 7.0 miles and a depth of 142 feet, this is the longest and deepest body of water within the park. It can also be the roughest. Unlike the other well-protected inland lakes, Siskiwit Lake has to be entered cautiously. Sudden squalls often blow across the Greenstone Ridge,

Mud Creek on the Island Mine Trail, west end of Siskiwit Lake.

creating choppy water with 2-foot waves and whitecaps.

It is a 3.5-mile paddle from Wood Lake to the portage to Malone Bay Campground. In ideal weather it might take you less than 2 hours or twice as long if the wind and waves are working against you. There are more than a dozen islands scattered throughout the lake, with most of them located at the east end. Ryan Island has the distinction of being "the largest island in the largest lake on the largest island in the largest freshwater lake in the world."

By staying along the south shore, you paddle through narrow gaps between two islands and the shoreline. The second is Eagle Nest Island, and it is a little over 0.5 miles east of the portage to Malone Bay.

Siskiwit Lake to Malone Bay Portage

Rating: easy
Distance: 0.2 miles

From Siskiwit Lake it is 0.25 miles to Malone Bay along a level, almost entirely planked trail that follows the stream between the lake and the bay for much of the way (see map on page 92). The trail splits off at one point,

Malone Bay Campground shelters.

and the lefthand fork leads off to the dock and ranger cabin. The other fork heads straight to the campground shelters.

Some paddlers are dropped off at Malone Bay (see Chapter 9), portage their craft over to Siskiwit Lake, and never go any farther the rest of the week. The reason for their contentment is the lake's fishing. The lake contains 17 species of fish, but is best known for having the only landlocked population of lake trout in the park.

Powerboats are not allowed on Siskiwit, but canoeists and kayakers will find conditions ideal to surface troll for lake trout. Pike and yellow perch can also be landed, especially among the many small islands at the east end. Some anglers prefer to follow the north shore and fish for brook trout in the streams that run off the Greenstone Ridge into Siskiwit Lake.

Many paddlers spend an extra day at Malone Bay Campground before heading back to Rock Harbor Lodge. Interesting day trips in the area include paddling around the islands in Malone Bay. Among them is Wright Island, to the west of the campground, where a fishing camp still stands.

For a combined hiking and boating trip, paddle to the west end of Siskiwit Lake. Here, the stream from Mud Lake empties out and is crossed by the Ishpeming Trail on a wooden bridge. It is only a 4.0-mile walk from here to Ishpeming Point and the lookout tower on the Greenstone Ridge (see Chapter 9).

In the northeast corner of the lake, 4.0 miles from the portage to Malone Bay, is a bay that leads to a small cove. In the cove is the portage trail to Intermediate Lake.

Siskiwit Lake to Intermediate Lake Portage

Rating: easy to moderate
Distance: 0.3 miles

The portage to Intermediate Lake is less than 0.5 miles long and traverses level and sometimes wet terrain. It leads straight for the lake and ends at a small inlet at the lake's western end.

INTERMEDIATE LAKE

The portages to Intermediate Lake, the only way to reach that body of water, are almost directly across from each other at the west and east ends. The lake is 1.0 miles long and has a depth of 24 feet. Yellow perch and northern pike are both found in its many coves and inlets.

As you paddle across the lake and approach the east end, you should see a large cove to the northeast. The cove is site of the portage trail to Lake Richie and the Intermediate Lake Canoe Campground. Both are marked.

Intermediate Lake to Lake Richie Portage

Rating: moderate
Distance: 0.6 miles

The trail begins with a gradual climb from the shoreline of Intermediate Lake until it skirts around a noticeable rock bluff. The path rounds the bluff and dips and climbs over rocky terrain before leveling out. The final portion is a sharp 30-yard drop to the shoreline of Lake Richie.

The trail emerges on the upper arm of Lake Richie. Almost directly across the lake is the marker for the Lake Richie Canoe Campground, which can be seen from the trail's end. The campground is on a hill that overlooks the western half of Lake Richie.

14 THE WEST END

*Siskiwit Bay • The South Shore • Rainbow Cove •
Grace Harbor • Washington Harbor*

Distance: 39 miles (Malone Bay to Windigo)
Portages: 1
Longest portage: 0.8 miles
Paddling time: 4–5 days

For kayakers who have open-water experience, the right equipment, and time, a paddle along the south shore of the Island, from Siskiwit Bay to Washington Harbor, can be a challenging adventure. The trip includes good scenery, solitude, and the Lady herself. There is something to be said for paddling Lake Superior where you have the Island's rocky coastline on one side and the lake's endless surface on the other.

In this stretch, kayakers have an advantage because there are no facilities for powerboaters, no access trails for hikers, and no protected

Kayaking the Island shoreline.

water for canoeists. Park rangers strongly recommend that canoeists not attempt the south shore. Lake Superior's sudden squalls and rough seas would quickly swamp an open craft such as a canoe. Though the south shore has more coves and beaches than the north side, emergency landings can still be tricky.

Unless you plan to paddle from Siskiwit Bay to Rainbow Cove in 1 day, a paddle that would take 12–16 hours in ideal conditions, it is necessary to obtain special permission from NPS park officials to camp in undesignated areas. This would allow you to break the long paddle into 2 or more days.

Kayakers should have tight-fitting storm skirts to prevent waves from flooding their boats. Preferably, they should also have plastic foam or other padding under their seat. Lake Superior can be cold, and you'll need something more than a couple of layers of fiberglass between your bottom and the water.

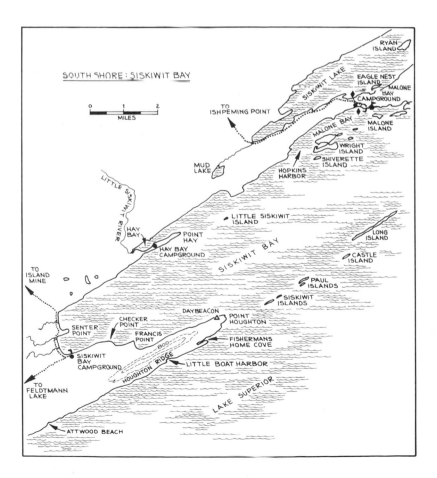

Although the paddle from Malone Bay to Washington Creek can be done in 2 days, it is best to plan on 4, with 3 days of paddling and an extra day for rough water. A good schedule would be to go from Malone Bay to Attwood Beach or Long Point the first night, to Rainbow Cove and Feldtmann Lake the second night, and on to Washington Harbor the third day.

At Washington Harbor it is foolhardy even for kayakers to continue on around the north shore. Once past Huginnin Cove the shore consists of steep cliffs and bluffs without adequate places to beach during rough weather. Old-timers generally agree that the north shore receives the worst that Lake Superior has to offer.

You can either end your trip at Washington Harbor or hop on *Voyageur* with your kayak and be transported to McCargoe Cove or the Five Fingers area (see Chapter 4).

SISKIWIT BAY

From Malone Bay Campground the paddling is easy for 2.0 miles as you head west through well-protected Malone Bay. Keep an eye out for moose on the small islands that border the bay or the old fish camp in one of Wright Island's protected coves.

Once you pass Wright Island you enter Siskiwit Bay, and the water will probably be noticeably rougher. The large bay is separated from Lake Superior by a thin reef that runs from Point Houghton for more than 7.0 miles to Menagerie Island. Although the reef breaks up Superior's surf and slow rollers, Siskiwit can still get surprisingly rough, with 3-foot waves and whitecaps possible any time; even 6 footers have been known to form on the bay.

From the west end of Malone Bay it is a 4.0-mile paddle to Point Hay and the beginning of Hay Bay. This narrow bay is well protected and a good place to hang out if Siskiwit Bay is kicking up.

Hay Bay Campground

Located toward the bottom half of the peninsula that forms Hay Bay is a small but pleasant campground. The site has a dock, pit toilet, and space for tents. There is also a short trail that leads across to the rocky shore of Siskiwit Bay.

At the head of the bay is the mouth of Little Siskiwit River, where there is fishing for brook and rainbow trout in the river's swift sections and deeper pools. Those with the time and the adventurous spirit can hike part way up the river to see numerous beaver dams and lodges.

At Hay Point, kayakers have an option either of paddling straight across to Point Houghton or following the shoreline of Siskiwit Bay to reach the same destination. The crossing from Point Hay to Point Houghton, a 3.0-mile paddle through open water, is a risky venture. In good weather, the

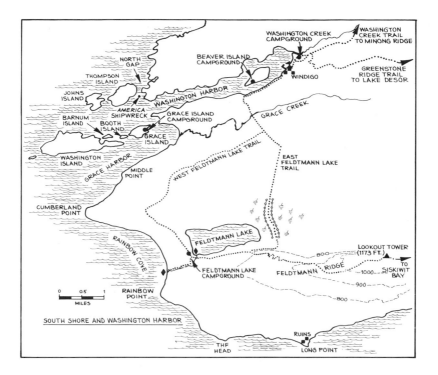

crossing takes 1½ –2 hours, and at one point you'll find yourself 1.5 miles from the nearest land. With the lake's (and the bay's) ability to kick-up suddenly, the risk is not worth the time saved by this shortcut.

A safer alternative is to follow the shoreline to the head of Siskiwit Bay, with the possibility of overnighting at Siskiwit Bay Campground, one of the park's more pleasant areas to pitch a tent. The swing along the shoreline to Point Houghton is a 9.0-mile paddle.

THE SOUTH SHORE

Once you paddle around Point Houghton and pass the day beacon at the tip of the peninsula, you are truly in Lake Superior. For most kayakers the entrance is accompanied by a tingle down their spine as they stare across the wide expanse of water in front of them. They are now in the world's largest freshwater lake.

You quickly pass several small coves, the third being Fisherman's Home Cove. Fisherman's Home is a good place to take a break because it offers well-protected water and Sam Rude's old fishing camp to investigate. Along with Rude's home, nets, and old wooden boats there are other huts. All buildings are private and should not be entered.

If the lake is calm, paddling this stretch in the afternoon can be a unique experience. With the sun sinking in the west, its rays will reflect off the water for an intense heat. You are cooled, however, by drops of water from Lake Superior that trickle off your paddle to your face and arms. Often, there will be a southwest wind gently pushing you from behind, and paddling becomes a series of effortless strokes.

The scenery along the South Shore is superb because you pass numerous small coves and inlets composed of red-pebble beaches. There are many spots where you can stop for the night, but the best are Attwood Beach and Long Point.

It is a 10.0-mile paddle from Fisherman's Home Cove to Long Point. Here, you will find long stretches of beach, many open spaces on the point, and the remains of a once thriving fishing camp.

From Long Point paddle toward The Head, 2.0 miles away. The Head is marked by a series of caves at the water level, some so large that you can paddle into them during calm weather. It takes a few paddle strokes before you round The Head and spot the tip of Rainbow Point.

RAINBOW COVE

The Head marks a change in direction as you swing north for a straight shot to Rainbow Point and the entrance to the prettiest cove on the Island. Stop for an evening, wander along Rainbow Cove's beaches, and enjoy the spectacular sunsets. At the southern end is the marked portage to Feldtmann Lake.

Rainbow Cove to Feldtmann Lake Portage

Rating: 0.8 miles
Distance: moderate

The trail head on the cove is 220 yards north of a stream that empties from Feldtmann Lake. The easy trail is surprisingly dry, considering the bog it passes through. It is level most of the distance except for a slight rise in the middle, where it swings away from the stream and drops to Feldtmann Lake Campground.

Kayakers should consider portaging their boats into Feldtmann Lake for early-morning fishing. The lake is renowned for its fine pike fishing but rarely sees any action beyond shore fishermen who hike in. With a kayak, anglers can fish the undisturbed middle or north-shore portions of the lake and have a good chance of feasting on fresh pike for breakfast.

GRACE HARBOR

From Rainbow Cove you can make a straight shot to Cumberland Point and paddle into the entrance of Grace Harbor, where Washington and

Grace islands give paddlers some protection from Lake Superior's large swells. The paddle from Rainbow Cove to Windigo can be accomplished in 3 hours in good weather. Those with an extra day can overnight at Grace Island Campground.

Grace Island Campground

The small campground has two shelters, pit toilets, and a dock. The view is nice from the shelters, and nearby is a sand spit that extends into the harbor.

Almost directly across from the campground on the Island is the mouth of Grace Creek, an ideal place to paddle in the evening to look for moose or fish for trout.

WASHINGTON HARBOR

From Grace Island you paddle north around Card Point and swing east into the mouth of Washington Harbor for Windigo. The harbor extends 3.0 miles and is broken up at its east end by Beaver Island.

Beaver Island Campground

This shoreline campground has three shelters, pit toilets, and a dock. All the shelters face the water, and there is a short trail that leads off to the west end of the island where you can view most of Washington Harbor. Often, when Washington Creek Campground is full of hikers, it is possible to get a shelter at Beaver Island.

There are many coves and inlets along the harbor. You can reach them by boat, and fish for brook or rainbow trout. Another interesting paddle in the area is to head west to the mouth of the harbor and then swing north through North Gap, which separates Thompson Island from the rest of Isle Royale. In North Gap, there is a buoy marking the sunken ship *America*, the passenger and freight steamer that sank June 7, 1928. One end of the ship lies only a few feet below the surface and can be easily viewed from the seat of a kayak.

Once past Thompson Island, you return to the open waters of Lake Superior on what is generally considered the roughest shoreline of the Island.

Isle Royale sunset.

AFTERWORD

Only the Moose and Wolves Can Stay

I sat in the Rock Harbor Lodge Restaurant, staring at my place setting. For the past six weeks I had used only a spoon, a metal bowl, and a set of hot-pot tongs. Now I had five pieces of silverware, two glasses, two saucers, a coffee cup, and a dinner plate in front of me—all for one meal.

Whenever you spend time in the woods, there is always an aftermath—that period when you readjust to a bed, hot showers, and civilization; that moment when you empty your pockets of lipsaver, Swiss Army knife, insect repellent, and matches and replace them with keys, a wallet, credit cards, and a watch; that brief transition when you leave the wilderness and re-enter the daily patterns of your life.

Whether your adventure is one week long or six, this is a quiet moment of realizations. At Isle Royale these moments are even more pronounced. For many backpackers the time to reflect is extended over a six-hour boat ride back to the mainland.

You swap stories and memories with other park visitors, laughs with another hiker, information with the NPS ranger on board. In one thought you wonder if your car will start after 14 days of being idle, and in the next you realize that yesterday you were in the woods.

At other parks and preserves you go from the trail to your car in 15 minutes. But the Island is special. By the very nature of being isolated from the mainland, it forces you to pause and think about your trip. It permanently freezes the finer moments in the back of your mind. The heavy pack and the blisters are forgotten. What you remember are the moose and twin calves that wandered through the campsite and the pair of loons that split the night air with their eerie laugh.

These images are forever with you. They are Isle Royale's way of beckoning you back across Lake Superior. They're the mystical lure of the Island.

BIBLIOGRAPHY

Janke, Robert A. and Nadine Janke. *The Wildflowers of Isle Royale National Park.* Houghton, MI: Isle Royale Natural History Association, 1962.

―――*The Birds of Isle Royale National Park.* Houghton, MI: Isle Royale Natural History Association, 1964.

Johnsson, Robert G. and Philip C. Shelton. *Wildlife of Isle Royale.* Houghton, MI: Isle Royale Natural History Association, 1982.

Lagler, Karl F. and Charles R. Goldman. *Fishes of Isle Royale.* Houghton, MI: Isle Royale Natural History Association, 1982.

Linn, Robert M. *Forest and Trees of Isle Royale National Park.* Houghton, MI: Isle Royale Natural History Association, 1973.

Oikarinen, Peter. *Island Folk.* Houghton, MI: Isle Royale Natural History Association, 1979.

Peterson, Rolf O. *Wolf Ecology and Prey Relationships on Isle Royale* (Scientific Monograph Series). Washington, D.C.: U.S. National Park Service, 1977.

Rakestraw, Lawrence. *Historical Mining on Isle Royale.* Houghton, MI: Isle Royale Natural History Association, 1965.

―――*Commercial Fishing on Isle Royale.* Houghton, MI: Isle Royale Natural History Association, 1968.

Shelton, Napier. *The Life of Isle Royale.* Washington, D.C.: U.S. National Park Service, 1975.

INDEX